"*Closeness in Student-Teacher Relationships* is a unique exploration of the connection between children and their teachers. Dr. Stearns poses questions that challenge the reader to use philosophical, sociological, and psychological thinking to make sense of the small world of the elementary school classroom. Through case studies, the reader enters two classrooms in search of possible answers to the human equation of classroom life."

- **Lesley Koplow**, *Founding Director of the Center for Emotionally Responsive Practice at Bank Street College, USA*

"*Closeness in Student-Teacher Relationships* leads educators through a series of questions aimed at troubling the seemingly straightforward idea that many of hold as an unassailable truth: that 'good' relationships are the heart of effective and transformative classroom practice for students and teachers alike. Stearns challenges us to think critically about what makes a relationship 'good' and to explore the boundaries of closeness and intimacy that emerge when we consider issues of power, agency, and choice in our instructional practice.

Framed by essential questions ('Can you be close to someone and want them to change?') and grounded in ethnographic research conducted in two urban elementary classrooms, *Closeness in Student-Teacher Relationships* provides both direct and indirect opportunities to consider the author's claims. Building on Stearns' established scholarly commitment to centering the voices of children in educational scholarship, this book features substantial insights into the meaning of relationships in school from the first-hand perspectives of young people shared through interviews, classroom observations, and student art. Each chapter closes with guided questions for reflective practice that further position this book as a high-impact tool for teacher professional development."

- **Sara A. Clarke-deReza**, Associate Professor and Chair of Education and Co-Director of the Cromwell Center for Teaching and Learning at Washington College

# Closeness in Student-Teacher Relationships

*Closeness in Student-Teacher Relationships* centers children's perspectives on closeness in the classroom while giving teachers questions they can consider toward cultivating more mutually affirming social and emotional dynamics. Despite many educators' best efforts, today's norms around relationship development can be excessively adult-first and inattentive to the wishes, needs, and desires of school-age children. This book looks beyond prescriptive methods for relationship development by modeling accessible practices for internal reflective work and deepened considerations of childhood agency and social power imbalances. Using firsthand observations and interviews in schools, relevant autobiographical perspectives, and a thorough yet accessible evidence base, author Clio Stearns prepares in-service teachers to explore their own vulnerabilities and challenge the prevailing notions of adulthood as a fixed state of knowledge and authority.

**Clio Stearns** is Associate Professor of Education at Massachusetts College of Liberal Arts, USA, and author of *Consent in the Childhood Classroom: Centering Student Voices Across Early Years and Elementary Education*.

# Also Available from Routledge Eye On Education

(www.routledge.com/k-12)

**Black Appetite. White Food. Issues of Race, Voice, and Justice Within and Beyond the Classroom**
Jamila Lyiscott

**Consent in the Childhood Classroom: Centering Student Voices Across Early Years and Elementary Education**
Clio Stearns

**Educators as First Responders: A Teacher's Guide to Adolescent Development and Mental Health, Grades 6-12**
Deborah Offner

**Learner Choice, Learner Voice: A Teacher's Guide to Promoting Agency in the Classroom**
Ryan L Schaaf, Becky Zayas, Ian Jukes

**Teaching as Protest: Emancipating Classrooms Through Racial Consciousness**
Robert S. Harvey, Susan Gonzowitz

**Supporting Student Mental Health: Essentials for Teachers**
Michael Hass, Amy Ardell

**Nurturing Students' Character: Everyday Teaching Activities for Social-Emotional Learning**
Jeffrey S. Kress, Maurice J. Elias

**Differentiated Instruction Made Practical: Engaging the Extremes through Classroom Routines**
Rhonda Bondie, Akane Zusho

**Closeness in Student-Teacher Relationships: Centering Children's Perspectives on Connection in the Classroom**
Clio Stearns

# Closeness in Student-Teacher Relationships

## Centering Children's Perspectives on Connection in the Classroom

Clio Stearns

Routledge
Taylor & Francis Group
NEW YORK AND LONDON

Designed cover image: Getty Images

First published 2026
by Routledge
605 Third Avenue, New York, NY 10158

and by Routledge
4 Park Square, Milton Park, Abingdon, Oxon, OX14 4RN

*Routledge is an imprint of the Taylor & Francis Group, an informa business*

© 2026 Clio Stearns

The right of Clio Stearns to be identified as author of this work has been asserted in accordance with sections 77 and 78 of the Copyright, Designs and Patents Act 1988.

All rights reserved. No part of this book may be reprinted or reproduced or utilised in any form or by any electronic, mechanical, or other means, now known or hereafter invented, including photocopying and recording, or in any information storage or retrieval system, without permission in writing from the publishers.

For Product Safety Concerns and Information please contact our EU representative GPSR@taylorandfrancis.com. Taylor & Francis Verlag GmbH, Kaufingerstraße 24, 80331 München, Germany.

*Trademark notice*: Product or corporate names may be trademarks or registered trademarks, and are used only for identification and explanation without intent to infringe.

ISBN: 978-1-032-99862-6 (hbk)
ISBN: 978-1-032-99762-9 (pbk)
ISBN: 978-1-003-60638-3 (ebk)

DOI: 10.4324/9781003606383

Typeset in Palatino
by SPi Technologies India Pvt Ltd (Straive)

*To Inanna*

*My apple, my pangolin, my ferocious lion
I feel so close to you.
Thank you for teaching me more about what that means.
I love you.*

# Contents

*Acknowledgements* . . . . . . . . . . . . . . . . . . . . . . . . . . . . . . . . . x

    Introduction. . . . . . . . . . . . . . . . . . . . . . . . . . . . . . . . . . . . 1

1   Can You Be Close to Someone and Still Be Yourself?. . . 23

2   Can You Be Close to Someone Who Has Power
    Over You?. . . . . . . . . . . . . . . . . . . . . . . . . . . . . . . . . . . . . 41

3   Can You Be Close to Someone and Be Very
    Different from Them?. . . . . . . . . . . . . . . . . . . . . . . . . . . 59

4   Can You Be Close to Someone Who Is Just the One
    You're With? . . . . . . . . . . . . . . . . . . . . . . . . . . . . . . . . . . 77

5   Can You Be Close to Someone and Want Them to
    Change? . . . . . . . . . . . . . . . . . . . . . . . . . . . . . . . . . . . . . 97

6   Can You Be Close to Someone Who Doesn't Want
    to Be Close to You?. . . . . . . . . . . . . . . . . . . . . . . . . . . 121

7   Can You Be Close to Someone When It Feels Like
    the World Is Ending?. . . . . . . . . . . . . . . . . . . . . . . . . . 141

# Acknowledgements

Writing this book has taken more honesty than I am used to, which is a bit embarrassing. That makes it sound like I am used to lying in my writing. I am not! It's just that this is more personal and introspective than I've gotten publicly, at least for a long time, and because of that, the people I want to acknowledge come from more different parts of my world.

First, I want to thank the teachers I feature in this book: Ainsley, Laila, and Benjamin. They opened their classroom doors to me on good and bad days, took time to really talk with me about their struggles, joys, and vulnerabilities, and helped me think about how I wanted to frame the ideas I was considering. Being a teacher is a lot of work as it is, and these three took on plenty extra when they let me in. Along those same lines, I want to thank the principals of their schools for being open to letting a researcher into the building. Most of all, though, I am grateful to the children in those classrooms for being so real with me, reminding me of so many things that matter, behaving both well and absurdly, and just showing up to do school, do life, do the seemingly impossible job of being a person among people.

I also feel grateful for Massachusetts College of Liberal Arts, where I have found my academic home. My colleagues at MCLA have such great senses of humor about our work, and my students there are always willing to practice making mistakes with me! In particular, I thank Dr. Maggie Clark, office mate, thinker, support, and friend extraordinaire. Maggie makes work a better place to be; I wish everyone had a colleague like her. I count myself fortunate to work in an education department where we can laugh and be humble just as much as we can cry and rant. My students also bring me into classrooms with them and remind me all the time what it means to do the daily work of teaching. I am especially grateful for those opportunities.

My editor at Routledge, Dan Schwartz, has been a consistent support. He has also, more recently, reminded me, for instance, that the words on a page and the realities they try to represent have the power and potential to outlast any particular political moment. I certainly hope he is right. I thank the entire Routledge team for being willing to help me bring this book to fruition.

This is a book about closeness and relationships, and writing it has made me think a lot about the people I am close with now, the people I have been close with in the past, and the people who have taught me what closeness is and isn't. For example, watching my children make their ways through childhood and adolescence gives me a different vantage point on what it is to go through days and days of school forming relationships. I've been grateful to the other characters – some parents, some teachers, some both – who are on this journey with them and with me. For example, I will never stop feeling thankful to Derek Shea, principal of Crocker Farm Elementary School, in Amherst, MA. Derek is just a remarkable school leader who knows about the absurdity and wonder of what goes on among children and between children and their teachers. Once, about four years ago, Derek told me that he respects my capacity to worry – and honestly, I haven't let that go as a message of help and hope in my hardest relational times. Kristen Ripley of Amherst Regional High School is a mom alongside me and also a teacher my children have been lucky enough to encounter, and she has shown me such an incredible combination of stoicism and vulnerability – and she's always there with a needle and thread, with photos of chickens and guinea pigs. Tracey Kaplan of Summer Street Preschool in Somerville, MA keeps reminding me that strong relationships don't have to mean sacrificing integrity and resistance. Jeff LeFebvre of Crocker Farm Elementary reminded me that an authentic relationship is actually nothing to sneeze at and can save a child's vision of himself and of school. Heather Sullivan-Flynn of Amherst Regional Middle School helped me learn by observing that the need to be treated like a four-year-old in a temper tantrum definitely doesn't end for children by the time they are fourteen! Farah Ameen, Ginny Hamilton, and Eugene Goffredo are parent friends who help me think about school with irony and show me different ways to know and care about the beautiful, bizarre children of our "village."

I'm grateful for my children's friends, who I won't list here by name out of respect for their privacy, partly because they are all sloppy, beautiful humans, and partly because they remind me so often of what is likely to matter most at any given moment in a child's day and journey. The people I also won't name are the counterexamples, the painful, forced, disrespectful, and mindless relationships I see people attempting with my children and those of others every day. I use those harsh adjectives but mean my gratitude sincerely, because I think those bumbles, too, help children find their way along and definitely offer as much education – in its broadest sense – as their more obviously positive and productive counterparts.

I am grateful to my in-laws, Richard Balkin and Felice Swados, whose presence in my life has remained steadfast, healing, and strong. Rick in particular is quoted in this book because I have found few people with wisdom on closeness as funny but true as his. I am also grateful to my family of origin, including my father, Peter Stearns, my mother, Carol Zisowitz, and my siblings, Duncan Stearns, Deborah Stearns, Wendy Katz, Julie Wiener, and Cordelia Stearns. From these people I got my earliest lessons about closeness, and I'm lucky that enough of our relationships are ongoing that I can think, laugh, and learn together with them in many meaningful ways.

My friend Emily Prabhaker is one of the people I know who is the least judgmental about the different ways a relationship can get funky and weird. I am thankful to Emily for being there for laughter and tears, for taking children seriously right next to me, but also reminding me that encountering closeness, and working through its complexities, doesn't end in this moment called middle age.

I have had a lot of mentors over the years, and their work echoes in mine whether or not I am citing them directly. In these roles, I am grateful to Dr. Paula Salvio, Dr. Jonathan Silin, and Dr. Harper Keenan, all of whom have taught me so much about writing and thinking about children. Even though this work is the least academic I have produced, it is informed by decades of reading, particularly in psychoanalysis, children's literature, and childhood studies, and I thank the scholars in those fields, dead and alive, who placed primacy on relationships as a way of understanding and surviving the world.

Still, most of all, I feel thankful for my family – they are right there, they put up with me, they mostly accept what I have to offer. My wife, Miranda Balkin, has weathered so many ups and downs of closeness with me over the years, and I don't know where I would be without her. Miranda also read and commented on these chapters in spite of not what I'd call a surplus of free time. I do really thank her for that, but not nearly as much as I thank her for being my person. On days that we are ships passing in the night (so many days like that!) I still just always know she is there – and that's not something I used to believe possible.

My son, Holden Stearns, sometimes seems to have a mind so different from mine that I can't believe we coexist in one species, much less one home. But Holden and I understand each other, and when I laugh with him, when I look into his beautiful eyes, when I hear him strum his guitar, see the pits he digs, and watch him struggle and celebrate, I feel granted this gift of intimacy with just an absolute gem of a human. Holden will get irritated at me for just about every word in that paragraph, but my god, do I feel close to him.

My daughter, Inanna Balkin, is a person who lives and loves so fiercely, and when she shows and tells me things about closeness, and even when she rightfully pulls away, I feel the wisdom of the ages right alongside the freshness of someone willing to take on the world with eyes wide open. We can drive around puzzling over any one of this book's questions together for hours, and she'll always surprise me with insight, power, and depth. She, too, will get irritated at me for these words, but she'll also laugh and nod, I think. This last year, my closeness with her has deepened and melded with a profound respect.

Miranda, Inanna, and Holden – I love you. Thank you for being my anchor and letting me anchor you! And thank you for helping me think about this book.

# Introduction

This book started at a difficult time for me in terms of relationships. I was navigating a years-long fallout with my mother and figuring out how to move forward with my sisters, who chose to remain close to her. That one sentence masks so much complexity: ambivalence, sadness, anger, and self-doubt, alongside pride, awareness, freedom, and newfound intimacy. Relationships are many things; simple is not one of them.

I started working on this book, in other words, because I was thinking about the relationships in my life and what they mean to me. I love a lot of people and have close connections, but I do not find closeness easy. As with anyone, some of this is based in my specific life history, some in my temperament, some in more recent priorities and values. Even that litany sounds more academic than what I mean. Fundamentally, I find closeness difficult because closeness *is* difficult – intense, rewarding, certainly important, and rarely straightforward.

The funny thing is, even though relationships are endlessly complicated and come with a seemingly infinite set of possible challenges, there is also a kind of cultural story about how easy and great they are. It takes a lot for most of us to be honest, even with ourselves, about what we struggle with in closeness. Admitting to these struggles can bring up all kinds of pain: traumatic family situations, sitting alone at the middle school lunch table, the end of a first romantic relationship. It is more fashionable to focus on the positive, and while this has its place, when we paint a picture of relationships as easy, we set up strange and unreasonable expectations for ourselves and others.

Most readers will already recognize that relationships are a huge part of teaching. They form inadvertently the moment two or more individuals collide in a classroom. A classroom becomes a web of human relationships intersecting messily day after day. The teaching world puts a lot of weight on these relationships. This is not inherently bad, but it is not always fair or true to what a human relationship is or can be. This book takes on the question of what classroom relationships might be about, whether and why they matter, and what they mean to children, whose voices are so often left out of conversations about their daily lives.

## Relationships and Classroom Management in My Teaching History

I started teaching elementary school in the early 2000s. From the beginning, the thing I struggled with most was classroom management. The children in my class liked me a lot, we had a lot of fun together, and our curriculum was engaging and creative, but they also did pretty much whatever they wanted all the time. This ranged from low-key infractions like constant callouts and interruptions to bigger and scarier problems. One of the many low points occurred when Gregory refused to get off the departing subway as we returned from a field trip as I stood, crying, blocking the door from shutting while an NYC transit employee looked at me with extreme disdain and pity, sizing Gregory up and telling him, "Get off my train now or ELSE." (Gregory listened right away.)

As I now believe to be true of most teaching problems, my classroom management challenges did not have so much to do with classroom management and, instead, were caused by deep conflicts in myself: Why don't people listen to me? Do I have the right to tell them what to do? I cannot lie and say that I have resolved these problems. Now, with college students, the struggles are different. They tend not to call out, but they don't put their phones away or get to class on time (and boy, do a lot of them like to pack up five minutes before we're done!).

Both then and now, when I tentatively raise these questions with colleagues, I encounter two different types of responses.

The first response is one I am more likely to get from seasoned and generally confident teachers or colleagues. They have pushed through burnout and found a way to make classrooms work for them. These answers tend to be around clarity of expectations, establishment of routines, and consistency of response. "Don't let them get away with that. Three strikes and you're out. Cell phone use during class means ten points off the day's participation grade." There is a massive amount of literature on classroom management following this school of thought, and what it comes down to are some moderately effective tips for making most groups of people comply with externally determined behavioral standards.

A separate kind of response comes from a more progressively minded group of educators and thinkers, critical of compliance-oriented classroom management. I have heard many educational thinkers of this mind actively chafe at the phrase "classroom management," saying that it implies a restrictive, teacher-centered, punitive approach. Thinkers along these lines (and I often count myself among them) put more focus on building strong classroom communities, pursuing justice in teacher/student interactions, co-regulating the expectations of the classroom alongside our students, and perhaps most of all, building strong relationships between students and teachers.

As ideas about "trauma-informed practice" and social and emotional learning have gained traction in education, relationships have played an increasingly central role. If you do a cursory internet search for pretty much any common classroom management issue, "develop strong relationships" is likely to come up as advice. When there is a good, close relationship between student and teacher, as the argument goes, the student is more motivated to try hard in school, to comply with behavioral expectations, and to meet the teacher halfway (Beatty-O'Ferrall et al., 2010). A teacher who has strong relationships with their students will reap the benefits of functional classroom management, but perhaps more importantly, will feel more satisfied and less burnt out at work (McCormick and Barnett, 2011).

This is exciting as part of a broader acceptance of a turn away from punitive discipline. But I have some problems with it too, even if they are difficult to admit. For one thing, there is a lot more superficial attention paid to authentic relationships between teachers and children than there is time, energy, or opportunity over the course of most rigidly structured school days for building and maintaining these relationships. Further, I am not sure how much I believe a relationship can be mandated or forced. Finally, I don't know how many children are actually that interested in relationships with their teachers, and school forces enough on children without forcing them into relationships they don't desire. These problems have led to some of the questions this book sets out to explore.

Despite instructions to develop strong relationships, from a range of sources disparate in tone and audience, there has been little written about what a genuine close relationship between student and teacher actually looks like. No research to date has examined children's own ideas about what it means to feel close to another person in school: whether children consider themselves to have strong relationships with teachers, what that means to a child, and whether it is desirable. Finally, there have been no honest examinations in the literature about what we are really asking of children and teachers when we mandate that they form relationships, and what kinds of explorations of interpersonal existence might be damaged by such a demand. This book seeks to close these gaps.

Many elementary teachers work valiantly to build strong relationships with children. Probably the biggest reason is that these relationships keep teaching gratifying and rewarding amid previously unthinkable external and internal pressures: everything from the terror of school shootings to the maddening grind of mind-numbing curricular mandates, from anxieties about punishments for teaching with supposedly controversial books to stress about the role of AI in teaching and learning. Certainly, I hear from my students again and again, just as I heard from the teachers in this study, it is the relationships with children that keep them going, that make them want to stay in an extremely difficult job.

During my first year teaching fifth and sixth grade, in the same class with Gregory of the subway debacle, I taught a boy named Will. Will was clever and socially savvy. He also understood that I was in over my head, and he was a pro at the thing some people call talking back. He finished his work quickly but with almost no effort, and he liked to do little bratty things: flinging erasers across the room, interrupting me mid-thought to point out every tiny error I made, letting me know quite explicitly that the work wasn't challenging enough for him. His way of behaving was hard for me to take, and eventually, I went to my principal about it. She listened carefully and handed me a five-dollar bill, instructing me to take Will out for pizza the next day at lunch, "and just get to know him."

I have told this story a lot of times to my own student teachers, because as infuriating as that advice was, it was also really helpful. Will and I had pizza together and came to a sort of peace. He liked that I got to know his hobbies and made more of an effort to emphasize his many strengths. Things calmed down a bit between us, and I did learn a really important lesson about teaching: how much it matters to take the time to see a child, to check the impulse toward fury or simple disbelief at what havoc a child can wreak.

But when I tell the story in a way that stops there, I also do a kind of disservice. Because the truth is, it was not a story with an *ending*. Will and I got a bit better together, and we did form a tentative relationship – sort of. He also kept doing all the same obnoxious things. They bothered me slightly less, and he was a little less inclined to bristle when I asked him for generosity with me and the classmates most likely to be bothered by conflict.

I was still completely relieved, though, when the year ended and I had a fresh start. I am pretty sure Will was every bit as relieved as I was.

It seems strange to put relationships into conversation with classroom management if you think about it carefully, because the purpose of a relationship isn't usually compliance or acceptance of the other's authority. Most teachers know that building relationships with children makes teaching more fun and rewarding, and that is no small thing. But that is different from relying on relationships to make the classroom function a particular way – and it makes me wonder if sometimes, "relationship" isn't *quite* the right word for what we are building.

For a long time, I have hesitated to articulate this concern because I worried it revealed something I in particular misunderstand about what relationships are or should be. I worry about this a lot, because building close relationships is something I have struggled with off and on throughout my life.

Increasingly, as I have met and worked with teachers of more and more different temperaments and styles, though, I have started to think that although I have struggles with closeness that are idiosyncratic based on my personality and life experience, the *fact* of struggling with relationships, with what it means to build and maintain one, is just part of being human. It is silly to pretend that because someone has a teaching license, or even decades of experience, they have cracked some sort of code on how exactly to exist in strong relation to others. That code does not exist. If it did, relationships would be boring, people would be homogeneous, and closeness when we do achieve it would not come with any special reward.

Maybe, in other words, my relationship with Will was imperfect, conflict-ridden, and complicated because that is how relationships are. Teaching might be less punishing if we could acknowledge some of the ways that teachers and children seek out truths about human experience in one another, test each other, and occasionally get really sick of being together. Adding "relationships" to the long list of things teachers have to do? That is a lot to ask. At the same time, of course, it is imperative, lovely, and rewarding. I am often not sure what to do at that crossroads.

I also find it troubling how little attention gets paid in teaching to how relationships with teachers can feel to children. What happens if a teacher is told to build strong relationships with their students, but some of the students have no interest in those relationships? By sanctifying relationships in classroom management, we replace one set of adult-oriented mandates (rules, routines, and discipline) with another (closeness and connection), one that might sound prettier but does no better at considering a day in school from the vantage point of a child.

To look at some of these questions and concerns more closely, I started exploring them alongside children and their teachers. Over the course of a school year, I spent time in two classrooms – a first grade and a fifth grade – in public schools, both in small cities in New England, investigating what it means to feel close to another person and whether children and teachers feel close to one another. Alongside this research, I reflected autobiographically on what closeness to another person might mean over the course of a lifespan; what helps me feel close to others, even across a power differential; and whether or why closeness is desirable.

In this book, I present the fruits of this research. What are teachers seeking from students when we say we are building relationships? What are some of the different things children think of when they say they feel close to another person? How do our own experiences with closeness and its obstacles impact our teaching?

I should note that I feel pretty close to the three teachers I worked with during this project, and that two of them are people I have known for many years, including throughout their teacher education at my institution. This is a new experience for me. Previous work I have done in classrooms has tended to be with teachers I know less intimately, and some of my writing,

I fear, has been disdainful of some of the classroom practices these teachers employed. This book is less critical and more curious about classroom life, and that is partly because the relationships I have with these teachers have helped me see their teaching moves more generously. I understand, too, that this can be read as a research bias, and I have tried to incorporate my usual critical lens. But an overarching love and trust for the teachers I was working with was helpful in understanding different ways their classrooms can feel for children, who also profess, overall, love and trust for them.

Ultimately, the book argues that mandates about relationship development pay insufficient attention to the wishes, needs, and especially worries of children. Adults in general, and teachers in particular, should focus less on applying specific strategies to relationship development and more on determining internally what we are seeking from other people in our lives.

I have come to believe that adults know less about what a relationship is, and what it means to be close to another person, than we mainly tend to pretend to in front of children. Why do we do this? This book encourages teachers to lean with me into their questions and internal struggles, rather than inadvertently but consistently deceiving children into believing that adulthood is a fixed, knowing, and settled state – that once you hit 24, 30, or 60, you know with certainty what it means to live and work alongside someone other than yourself. The book also describes some institutional obstacles to strong relationships between students and teachers or in schools overall. Rather than make recommendations for removing those obstacles, I show how children benefit from structures that allow them to operate under the radar, even against the rules of what school puts forth.

The teachers and pre-service teachers I work with feel great pressure to form strong relationships with the students in their classes. When something doesn't feel right about how the school day is panning out, they are quick to blame themselves for not understanding how best to relate to specific children, often, in turn, as a path toward getting those children to behave a certain way. The children I spoke with in this study mainly felt fine about their relationships with their teachers, but they also found this matter significantly less pressing than other ones, like connecting with their friends or "getting smarter." I hope this book helps start a conversation about what it means to explore relational closeness mutually with children, and to push the conversation about relationship development away from an instrumentalist perspective on relationships as just one more key to compliance. I also want to show you how complexly children are thinking about the relationships in their lives and how much awareness they are holding about what it means to connect to another person.

## How to Use this Book

This book introduces you to two classrooms of teachers and children who are doing their best to make things work together. It also takes you through some more personal explorations of why and whether relationships are complicated. The book is about closeness, but it is also about how difficult and knotty closeness can be. Because of that, one idea I will come back to again and again is the value of uncertainty. To me, uncertainty is a much-needed humility in teaching, something easy to lose track of when we as teachers are forced into a position of defending our professionalism and expertise. Public-facing teachers need to be sure about our practices, or we risk losing what little political and economic foothold we have. This is a private-facing book, though, and it asks you to relinquish that particular performance of confidence. I will try to do the same.

Because this book values uncertainty, it is not going to tell you exactly what you should do to form good relationships in your classroom. No such universal strategy or technique exists, because relationships are a lot more complicated than that and elude most kinds of mandates. Prescriptions based on certainty lead to a lot of shame when they don't work out exactly as described. Shame isn't necessarily bad, but in teaching, it can lead to a sense of deception – an imposter syndrome – and undue resentment between teachers and children that gets in the way of curiosity and growth. We say to ourselves, "Well, I used all the right techniques, and things still aren't working – it's because that particular kid is (bad, entitled, obnoxious, mentally ill, spoiled, traumatized, hopeless, etc)." No one wins under this kind of thinking.

Instead of tips, strategies, or advice, this book is going to give you a lot of different questions to think about. I recommend using it as a starting point for internal exploration. I try to be vulnerable in my writing: open about some of my own challenges in relationships, and willing to consider the flaws in my perception. This level of vulnerability is hard-won for me, but I hope it offers relief to teacher readers who might be questioning their feelings about how relationships unfold in the classroom. So the first way to use this book is by following its explicit and implicit questions and taking some time to think about them within yourself or with trusted colleagues.

The second way I hope you use this book is by attending carefully to what the children in my study offer. Two classrooms of children cannot be taken to stand in for children everywhere, but their words and ideas offer a general notion of how the relationship mandate might look from the child side of the equation. Many of the children in this study remind us about ways the same kinds of questions about closeness and connection repeat throughout the lifespan. I am inclined to think that anything that reminds adults, particularly teachers, how similar we actually are to children, leads to more forgiveness, patience, and compassion toward ourselves and the others in our world.

## How This Book Is Structured

While I was researching in classrooms, and while I was thinking about my own complicated web of relationships with others, what kept coming to me were questions. For the most part, these were questions about the different fears or worries one person might have entering into relationships with another. These are fears that relationship instructions generally don't take seriously enough, but they are serious fears that people grapple with in different ways over the course of their lives.

None of the questions I started thinking about has an absolute answer. For this reason, the book leans heavily on the significance of uncertainty, something I refer to as ***teaching without being sure***. I want to remind you that it is not only all right, but helpful and enriching, to accept a state of not knowing. Just like you might tell a child you do not know the answer to a question in geography or science, you can also admit that just because you are a teacher, you do not know everything about existing in relation to others.

Teaching without being sure is a vulnerable but honest version of teaching, something we tend to be defensive about because of how hard we have to work to be taken seriously as professionals. I understand that, but teachers' insistence that we understand what relationships are is deceptive. Children see this better than adults sometimes admit it, even to ourselves. Showing my own uncertainty as best as I can, I encourage teacher readers to consider my questions, but also develop your own, and be honest with children about the challenges inherent to the human condition.

Each chapter, then, takes on a particular question as it relates to the teachers and children I researched, as well as my own questions about relationships and closeness. Chapter 1 explores what it means to try to hold on to yourself while you are in a close relationship with another person, and Chapter 2 asks whether you can be close to someone who has power over you. In Chapter 3, I look at whether you can be close to someone and disagree with them or be very different from them. Chapter 4 explores the role of proximity in closeness: What does it mean when the people you feel closest to are not the ones right there? In Chapter 5,

I look at whether you can be close to someone and want them to change, and in Chapter 6, I wonder whether you can be close to someone who does not want to be close to you.

Chapter 7 looks at the many ways outside social and political forces can play out in classroom relationships, asking, can you be close to someone when it feels like the world is ending? This closing chapter recognizes the temptation to think of closeness as a guard against external pain and anxiety. Pulling together several of the observational anecdotes from throughout the text, I urge readers to face uncertainties about the world just as they face uncertainties about relationships and about teaching, but also to listen authentically and emergently to what children are saying – not just about what they want from school and relationships in school, but also about what they want the world to be and what they want their teachers to do toward making change.

## Theoretical Underpinnings

I am an academic, but this book does not aim to be an academic text. There are, though, theoretical approaches that underlie the work, and I encourage you to explore them more deeply. The first is that of Gert Biesta (2014, 2017, 2019, 2022), whose works consistently argue against the "learnification" of education. Biesta's philosophy reminds us that teaching is about more than learning and cognitive development. He describes one purpose of education as "grownupness," but is quick to argue for a unique definition of the concept. A young child can be as grown up as a chronological adult in this definition.

To be grown up, Biesta explains, is to understand how to live fully in the world without seeing one's self as the *center* of the world. Grownups take themselves, their identities, their needs and values seriously, but they also recognize that other ways, other priorities, are possible and rich. Grownups do not deny themselves or the seriousness of the conditions and problems that surround them. They want to be part of a society, they want to coexist. They also know that there are always going to be a range of value systems, and that coexistence sometimes means putting one's own priorities temporarily aside.

For Biesta, school can be a place where we all work toward and on grownupness together – but this can only happen when we remember that not everything is oriented toward more successful early literacy, more advanced and efficient higher math. I draw on Biesta as I show the different ways children are capable of conceptualizing relationships and mutual life. I also show how defensive structures in education, often rooted in what Biesta calls learnification, can force teachers into a problematic position of performed certainty that is not true to our internal sense of the world.

This book also draws heavily on Bronwyn Davies' (2016) work on emergent listening. Davies argues that listening to children can be a creative act, one that teaches adults about ourselves and the world around us and can lead us into ways of thinking and being that we were previously unprepared for. Emergent listening, for Davies, is by its nature an interpersonal process, and I draw on this line of thought as I show how teachers and children seek things from each other when we think about what it means to exist in relationship. I also aspire to draw on Davies methodologically as I describe my experiences listening to the children in this text.

Further, the book borrows significantly from Jonathan Silin's work (1995, 2016, etc.). Over the course of his distinguished scholarly career, Silin has consistently worked with the idea that children and adults have a great deal to gain from attentive, mutual coexistence and striving for honesty and vulnerability. Silin has argued that life includes repeated engagement with a range of existential questions, and that these do not look as different in early childhood and old age from how developmentalists might frame things. I draw on this approach consistently as I remind readers that teaching without being sure is sometimes a richer, if more difficult, approach than maintaining a pretense of certainty.

Finally, the book takes seriously the role of intersectional identities and how they play out disparately in education. At various points, I consider the impact on relationships of unconscious racial bias (e.g. Benson and Fiarman, 2019). I wonder about the ethics of requiring relationships from children who, for reasons related to cultural difference and racialized power structures, might simply not be interested in relationships with the largely white teaching corps at their schools.

I also consider the impacts of gender, gender identity, socioeconomics, disability, and the intersections among these identities on teacher relationships with students. Age and development are the central aspects of identity the book considers, and it would be false to pretend that it is a book primarily about the other identities so necessarily prominent in educational conversations oriented toward justice. At the same time, it is crucial to acknowledge the interplay among all of the aspects of children's and teachers' identities, and their awareness of how these identities play out in the world around them, as they impact classroom management and classroom relationships.

## The Classrooms in This Book

Over the course of the book, you will learn a lot about the daily rhythms of both classrooms, their teachers, and some of the children that inhabit them. Here, I aim to offer just an introduction to the teachers, their articulated philosophies, and the general demographics of both classrooms.

### Ainsley and Her Classroom

The first classroom where I conducted research was Ainsley Robyns' first grade. Ainsley was in her second year of teaching and her first at the school where I worked with her. When Ainsley started college, her goal was to become a pediatrician. She quickly learned that her heart wasn't in medicine, but she still wanted a career that would allow her to spend plenty of time with children. "I decided to try out teaching," she described, "and I found my purpose in that. My whole life changed. I know it sounds corny, but teaching has helped me grow into my own person."

Though she is early in her career, Ainsley plays a leadership role at her school, advocating for curriculum changes and organizing special events. In many of our conversations, Ainsley described *love* as central to her teaching. She wants students to know they are loved. She wants them to know that no matter what they bring to the classroom, she will love them and be there for them.

Ainsley teaches at a preK–6 public school in a small city in Massachusetts. The school is majority white (about 80%). According to Massachusetts data from 2023, about 90% of the students at the school come from low-income families. At one point during the school year, Ainsley estimated that more than half of her students were in foster care. There are a variety of reasons for this, but a significant one is the ravages of the nationwide opioid epidemic on an underfunded, underserved corner of the overall wealthy state.

In response to statewide demands for increased test scores at Ainsley's school, which is broadly underperforming and where only 20% of the students are estimated to read at grade level by third grade, the district decided three years ago to begin departmentalizing in first grade. This means that each child has two teachers: one who works on math and a bit of science, and one who teaches English Language Arts and a bit of social studies. Ainsley is the first grade ELA teacher. Functionally, this means that she meets with her "home base class" for about half an hour total out of the day for breakfast, morning meeting, and a closing circle. She also teaches them ELA for a full morning, and then she teaches ELA to the other class in the afternoon while her home base heads to her partner teacher for math. This kind of departmentalization in primary grades is becoming increasingly common, particularly in high poverty districts in spite of a lack of evidence about any benefits on student learning or well-being (Shanahan, 2021).

Physically, Ainsley's classroom is warm, busy, and bright. She has a small meeting area with an easel, a carpet, and bins of picture books. The front of the classroom contains clusters of desks with name tags that flip depending on which group is in the room. She has a smartboard, and Chromebooks for each student. The walls are decorated mainly with student artwork and posters about reading strategies. Ainsley also has a paraprofessional in her room most of the time, though the specific individual has changed many times throughout the year.

Ainsley, a white woman, came to teach where she does specifically because she has lived in the community her whole life and wanted to teach where she came from. Her first teaching job was in a smaller, more rural school further from home, and though she enjoyed it, she often felt distant from her students' lives. Going to after school events and connecting with families was challenging. Ainsley puts so much into her teaching; she is often the one organizing Career Weeks, game nights, and family breakfasts. She goes out of her way to develop connections to her students' caregivers as well as to colleagues across grade levels.

Curricularly, Ainsley is mandated to follow a scripted "science of reading" program called ReadyGen (published by the company formerly known as Pearson) along with the Fundations phonics/phonemic awareness program, Lexia for independent student work, and ThinkRSD for writing. This is a lot of mandates, and Ainsley describes herself as "still figuring out" how to do everything she is supposed to do but also "have some fun" teaching her six and seven-year-old students to read. She estimates that she spends about four hours every weekend going over the books of what she is meant to do in the coming week and trying to plan accordingly, but she hopes this will get easier with time, "If the district doesn't decide to change it up and buy all new programs!"

Most days, Ainsley has her whole group doing the same thing at the same time. She usually starts with a direct instruction period where students work on particular decoding or writing strategies: sorting digraphs, sounding out blends, spelling and writing sentences using sight words. She moves into independent work where students practice different skills or play related games, and she circulates for support and additional instruction. She often closes with a picture book read aloud and related discussion.

Once a week, when a special educator and an occupational therapist push into Ainsley's classroom, she has students work in stations on differentiated activities. She thinks this kind of differentiation is helpful for everyone but does not find it possible without additional adult support. Normally, Ainsley follows the same rhythm with both of her groups on any given day, though with her home base class, she often has more time for community-building activities that aren't part of the curricula.

Ainsley is a teacher with a lot of articulated visions and beliefs about teaching, and many of these beliefs are directly connected to how she builds and perceives relationships with students. These will become clearer over the course of the book, but the central philosophy Ainsley described again and again, and showed in words and behavior, is that teaching has to do with helping children feel and believe that they are loved. "I needed a lot of love as a child," she told me, "so I always think about how I can show each of them love in the way that is best for them."

## Laila, Benjamin, and Their Classroom

The second classroom where I worked was Laila Audrey and Benjamin Thatch's fifth grade. Laila, a white person who identifies as genderqueer but uses she/her pronouns in her teaching life and wanted me to use she/her pronouns in this book, was in her second year of teaching, and Benjamin, a white cisgender man, in his ninth, when I worked in their classroom.

Laila has always felt she wanted to be a teacher. She grew up working as a summer camp counselor and in after-school theater programs for children, often the same programs she had attended when she was younger. She describes herself as feeling "most at home" with children. Benjamin came to teaching because one of his childhood mentors was his seventh grade teacher, and as he grew up, he felt a strong desire to replicate and repay what she did for him. He started his career at a middle school and started to feel burnt out after a few years. A friend suggested working in a younger grade, and now he feels content there and especially happy in a co-teaching environment.

Laila and Benjamin work in a public school in a slightly bigger city than Ainsley's – the biggest city in their region. Their school is committed to an inclusive model of education. Every class in the building is team-taught by a teacher with an elementary license (in this case, Benjamin) and a teacher with a license in "moderate disabilities" (Laila). Children with IEPs are educated alongside typically developing peers, and a range of special educators and therapists spend time in different classrooms over the course of the week. Very rarely are children pulled out of their classrooms for services.

In Laila and Benjamin's class, 8 of the 19 students have IEPs, for a range of diagnoses including mild learning disabilities, ADHD, and moderate autism. Their classroom is more diverse than Ainsley's in other ways as well. Ten of their students are Latinx, one African American, and the rest white. The socioeconomic backgrounds of their students are more mixed, with 60% of the school qualifying for free and reduced lunch. Benjamin and Laila did not know of any students in their class who had ever been in foster care.

Probably because their school is considered a "choice" school within their district, the test scores there are a bit higher than at Ainsley's school (just under half of the students test on grade level in both reading and math). This, combined with a supportive, thoughtful, and strong-willed principal, means that although Laila and Benjamin are still beholden to district curriculum mandates, they have more flexibility than Ainsley about how to implement them. Laila and Benjamin also teach all of their students all day.

I have known Laila, like Ainsley, since she started her undergraduate degree. She was interested right away in working on this project. At first, Benjamin wanted to stay on the sidelines and was willing but a bit nervous about my observations, but then he decided he would join our interviews and be equally part of the project. This afforded me a great opportunity to learn more about co-teaching.

Laila and Benjamin's fifth grade is bustling and dynamic. The room is open and well-lit, with only student work and subject area anchor charts on the walls. Each student has a desk, but I rarely saw students sitting there. Instead, they sat around tables working with one of their teachers, on cozy cushions in a back corner of the room, or sprawled across mats in the hallway, getting work done quietly. Laila and Benjamin keep whole group lessons short, and most of the day in their classroom involves rotations through different small groups. They use a digital timer and a Smartboard to help students keep track of where they are and what they are doing.

**Overview of My Methods**

Before starting research in both of the classrooms, I obtained consent from all participating teachers, principals, and superintendents. I interviewed only children whose guardians consented. Out of Ainsley's two classes, this came to 12 children; in Laila and Benjamin's, there were 14. I also made sure each participating child assented before our interviews. I conducted observations in both classrooms during normal classroom activities, largely just to get a sense of their rhythms and a read on how the children and teachers appeared to relate to one another in real time. I interviewed all of the teachers several times – some interview sessions more formal than others – and also debriefed my observations with them. I spent about 30 minutes with each child interviewee, though this time frame varied based on the interest of the child. When children were willing, I also had them draw pictures to represent close relationships at schools.

It was from the combination of these observations, interviews, and drawings, alongside autobiographical reflection and informal conversations with a range of other teachers and teacher candidates, that I settled on the questions that organize this book's chapters. Notably, though at first glance first graders and fifth graders may seem to be at drastically different developmental moments, I found that the individual differences among children were more important than the four-year age gap in determining the different kinds of ideas and answers they put forth. Overall, I will discuss the classes and their teachers together as groups of people, rather than representatives of specific stages.

Closeness is beautiful, central to human life, something most of us want for ourselves and the people we love. Also, it is hard. The ways teachers and children relate to one another both reflect and affect the other relationships all parties involved have in their worlds. Increasingly, I believe and will show through this book that relationships cannot be reduced to mandates in the name of either better classroom management or stronger classroom communities. If there is one message I hope you take from this book, it is that the only certainty in the relational landscape of teaching is its steadfast uncertainty. Try not to be sure about what it means to manage a classroom, to relate to a child, to engage in best practice, to "be a good teacher." Teaching without being sure is as scary as it is freeing, as paradoxical as it is honest, but I am convinced that it is authentic. It is a way for adults to be true with children about how complicated it is to make your way to adulthood and through this frightening, lovely world.

## References

Beatty O'Ferrall, M. E., Cary, J., and Chen, D. W.. "Teaching Strategies That Prepare Students to Think Critically." *Education Digest* 76, no. 2 (2010): 32–39.

Benson, Tracey, and Fiarman, Sarah E.. *Unconscious Bias in Schools: A Developmental Approach to Exploring Race and Racism*. Cambridge, MA: Harvard Education Press, 2019.

Biesta, Gert. *The Beautiful Risk of Education*. London: Routledge, 2014.

Biesta, Gert. *The Rediscovery of Teaching*. London: Routledge, 2017.

Biesta, Gert. *Obstinate Education: Reconnecting School and Society*. Leiden: Brill Sense, 2019.

Biesta, Gert. *World-Centred Education: A View for the Present*. London: Routledge, 2022.

Davies, Bronwyn. *Politics of the Subject: Politics of the Performative*. London: Routledge, 2016.

McCormick, Meghan, and Barnett, Raymond. "Teachers at the Wheel: Using Inquiry to Drive Change." *Phi Delta Kappan* 92, no. 6 (2011): 42–45.

Shanahan, Timothy. "What Constitutes Evidence in Reading Research?" *Reading Research Quarterly* 56, no. S1 (2021): S129–S138. https://doi.org/10.1002/rrq.402

Silin, Jonathan G. *Sex, Death, and the Education of Children: Our Passion for Ignorance in the Age of AIDS*. New York: Teachers College Press, 1995.

Silin, Jonathan G. *Early Childhood, Aging, and the Life Cycle: Mapping Common Ground*. New York: Palgrave Macmillan, 2016.

# 1

# Can You Be Close to Someone and Still be Yourself?

When I was growing up, my family kept our peanut butter in the refrigerator. I don't know why. It was hard to spread because of how solid it turned in there, but peanut butter does taste good cold. Once, in high school, I was at a friend's house and we needed a snack. I watched her go into the pantry and pull peanut butter from a shelf, and I asked, wouldn't it be rotten? She laughed at me and we happily dipped pretzels in, and I liked it fine, but it still seemed strange. Many years later, living with roommates for the first time, I brought peanut butter home from the store and wondered about the right way to keep it. (I settled on the cabinet, and I have never looked back.)

I think about where to keep peanut butter a lot because of how confusing it can feel when you have a way of doing things – something you got from your family, something that you figured out on your own – and then you care about someone who thinks your way is strange or even wrong. This happens to children all the time in school as part of the excitement of encountering new people and spaces and experiences. It can also be scary.

That fear is particularly acute in a cultural context that tends to value individualism, placing a premium on separation and independent identities. It is possible to feel genuinely threatened by little, surprising differences because of how they accumulate to feel like an affront to your selfhood, your family's way of doing things, your sense of where you fit and how others perceive you. How do I know if I really like peanut butter at room temperature in some essential way, or if I had to make that change to connect with my friends better?

These same small, concrete questions unfold at profound levels and abstractions. Can a child maintain her identity as a devout Muslim and be close to a teacher who is Christian? Can a child from a family of political conservatives figure out and stay true to his own value system and also become close to a radically progressive teacher (a question underlying some of the culture war panic at play in parent vs. school educational debates in the US right now)? What does holding onto one's self mean about one's love for, closeness with, and willingness to trust another?

The question this chapter explores is about these small, and sometimes larger, affronts to individual identities and what can happen when they play out in a classroom. What happens when a child, for any number of reasons, does not want to give up any bit of themselves in pursuit of closeness to the teacher?

There are two different simple versions of the answer to this puzzle. The first simple answer admits, yes, children have to relinquish something to exist in healthy relation to their teachers and peers. That is part of what happens when kids go to school: they learn from their teachers and accept many of their teachers' ways of doing things. Sometimes, that means giving up ways they have done things before. They might have to learn to eat room temperature peanut butter (or, in many schools, no peanut butter at all!), to make the sound /b/ when they see a letter "b," to sit quietly for twenty minutes at a stretch. They might have to pledge allegiance to a flag, stop playing when it is time to officially "learn," eat and drink on a schedule they did not choose, wipe their noses with Kleenex when they drip, or plan out writing projects in a particular, formulaic way. This all serves the project of education.

This is a pragmatic argument and has merit. It can be important to help bring people out of the ways they have always done things, or to explore new possibilities that often come from a teacher's ways. I worry, though, that this approach leads to a sense of antagonism and fear between children and teachers that is not always conducive to a meaningful coexistence. A child might decide, "It's just not worth it to try to listen to you if you are going to make me forget myself." I worry even more about the shame children feel when they notice something about themselves that does not match their teacher, but feel they cannot or do not want to change this part of their identity. This child might decide, "Something is wrong with me because I cannot or do not want to do things the way my teacher does."

The second simple argument is sort of the opposite, and while I see this one more often in progressively minded, purportedly child-centered education circles, it is deceptive in its confidence. This argument holds: A loving, justice-minded teacher does not ask children to let go of themselves. We can be close to one another and make space for everyone to be themselves. In this argument, one person gets to chill their peanut butter, and the other leaves it out. No one comments on the oddness of the other person's affinities; if they do, it is to celebrate the excitement and richness of difference.

This argument sounds lovely to me at first. What I worry about here is the strong capacity I have noticed in certain styles and temperaments of children for finding the limits of adults' professed tolerance. I consider this hunt for sneaky adult limitations inevitable for many children and quite beautiful, but I think children once again often find themselves engulfed in shame or mistrust when they are told "your teacher celebrates your difference" but clearly notice that there is a point when this is no longer true. It can widen an undiscussed chasm between children and adults.

Also, it is the same intense defense of an individual's desire and right to hold onto their self that has contributed to a rise in homeschooling and an increased mistrust in the collective, communal project of public schools. This is the side of the coin that says, "If I don't believe in vaccines, and school requires them, then school is not for me and it is not for my child. If I believe in the New Testament as doctrine, and school does not, then school is not for my child. I will not enter a situation that requires me to even slightly question what I believe to be certain, true, and inherent to my identity." The same defense of self that can seem progressive and creative also defends a betrayal of community, reverting to a very individualistic vision of education that I think few teachers really hope to see.

Teachers are better positioned to consider the surprising aspects of self that children bring into a classroom if we stay away from simple arguments and immediate, pat answers – especially answers that invite dichotomy. Instead, we should acknowledge the ways that question plays out across relationships: the fact that it is a knotty one that maybe we are all thinking about together, and children are also exploring in our absence. When teachers ask children for trust, we are asking for their belief that we can be close to them without taking from them, without asking that they deny the norms of their families or that nugget of self they have ascertained and are learning to hold dear. Can children genuinely be themselves in school and feel connected to their teachers? I am not sure; the rest of this chapter asks you to think openly about this question along with me.

## Jordan Is a Bear

*First-grade Jordan has decided to be a bear today. When I get to his class, I see him sitting in the back corner of the meeting area while Ainsley works through a phonological awareness activity with the class. Jordan is sitting like the rest of the children, but while several of his classmates look up at me and wave, he glances in my direction and paws at the air.* Ainsley smiles at me and motions to a chair where I can sit, and I watch the children as they sort words by their beginning sounds, ch or sh.

After a few more minutes, Jordan lies on the ground and starts to roll back and forth. On his back, he lifts his arms and legs to the air and stretches, emitting a kind of rumbling sound. On his front, he pokes his head up, eyes darting back and forth. The other children pay no mind. While I'm trying to tell if they are inadvertently oblivious or intentionally ignoring him, I see Ainsley put her pointer down and turn her attention to Jordan.

"Jordan," Ainsley says in her characteristically quiet voice. She gets up and walks through aisles among the children's bodies. Most of them watch her. Ainsley squats low to the ground and taps Jordan on his shoulder as he rolls back and forth, pawing the air more aggressively and clearing a path around him. He looks at her and growls. "I'm a bear," Jordan announces. Several children giggle, and Micah starts rolling on the floor too; since he is a lot bigger than Jordan, this causes more disruption.

Ainsley's voice stays very soft. "Jordan," she says again, "I need you to look at me. I need your blue eyes to meet my brown eyes."

"But I'm a BEAR," Jordan rumbles, now looking at Ainsley.

"I hear you, Jordan," Ainsley says, "you might feel like being a bear today, but your eyes need to find my eyes and you need to take one big breath in and one big breath out. If you're acting like a bear, you can take a little break in the hall with Ms. Severson and come back once you're ready to learn, but the rest of my friends –" and Ainsley gestures to the room, "the rest of our friends, they are here for reading now and I want them to be able to focus and hear my different sounds." Jordan gives one more tiny growl but sits up quietly for the rest of the lesson.

## Holding on to Yourself

What is it that makes a six-year-old become a bear during a reading lesson, then make the tremendous compromise of turning back into a human child? Part of the power of children's play is precisely in its mystery, so easily diminished by adult attempts at analysis. Perhaps Jordan was simply seeing what might happen if he was something very different today. Jordan did not say, "I'm pretending to be a bear" or, in Ainsley's translation, "I am acting like a bear." He said, "I am a bear," and he waited to see where that landed. What he found out was, he can't be a bear and also be part of Ainsley's lesson.

All of the time I spent observing in Ainsley's classroom, I was struck by the tenderness with which she related to her students, and by the trust they seemed to grant her in turn. Her students follow her through reams of curriculum, assessment after assessment, dance parties and pancake breakfasts. In interviews, Ainsley's students spoke consistently about how much they love her, how close they feel to her and how deeply they trust her. Her response to Jordan is filled with empathy. She gets right to his level and honors his feelings, giving him choices and taking the whole interaction at his pace, keeping her tone loving and compassionate. They have a moment of connection, eye to eye, breathing with one another. But Jordan is also interested in the limits of that connection. "Will my teacher still love me, still let me be here, if I am a bear?"

It is aspirational to say, in a classroom, we honor one another's differences; your teacher can love you and still let you "be yourself." Teachers have a powerful level of influence, though, over who a child's self can and cannot be. That is part of the point of being a teacher. It also makes for a precarious dynamic in relationships. Ainsley seems to pick up on Jordan's playing around with individuation when she emphasizes their different eye color, but she wants to bring him back to her non-bear orbit, and so she has them breathe together. Is Jordan calmed? Is he making an appropriate, necessary compromise, something that contributes to his and others' education? Or is he making a scary sacrifice?

The compliance teachers generally look for in a classroom, and for that matter what those in power look for in any society, requires some denial of impulse and desire. We cannot simply listen to the inner beat of what we want all the time; it would cause havoc and suffering. It would be difficult to teach a first-grade classroom filled with bears and piglets and unicorns. We can have different eye colors, but we can't really learn to read together if we belong to different species. Moreover, selves are fluid – not only in childhood but throughout the lifespan – so a claim that children bring static identities to schools doesn't make sense.

At the same time, Jordan's growls and subsequent compromise raise a question about what a child has to do to be in a good relationship with their teacher. One answer is that we ask many children to relinquish quite a lot of themselves when we ask them to enter into such a relationship, the thing teachers are counseled to create in the name of good classroom management. This is not necessarily bad. The problem is in the pretense of honoring individuality when actually a lot of relationships require more give. "Be yourself," school tells kids like Jordan, "just don't be a bear."

How many of us have had to think about keeping track of ourselves in close relationships with others? I think of my old friend, Basil, someone I have loved since the day we met in matching purple denim shorts on the bus ride to sixth grade. It was probably more the matching anxiety about middle school than the twin shorts that brought us together, but I spent so much of the first decade of our friendship emulating Basil, who always seemed to know himself so well. Basil understood cool music, great books, adolescent social dynamics, and interesting ideas. I loved what he loved.

Even today, both of us in our 40s, I find myself rethinking my opinions and values when I talk to Basil. A few months ago, he told me how in his fight for affordable housing in his city, he has started protesting a housing organization – also seemingly progressive – where another friend works. The protests have been painful and disruptive, and I know how much our other friend believes in her job and its role in getting more housing built for those who need it most. Frankly, I think she knows more about the topic than Basil – but he is confident and persuasive, and I forgot what I had learned from her and also what I personally believed about the topic while I listened to Basil passionately describe his work. I genuinely forgot myself! Honestly, I sometimes still feel such a connection to him that I'm not sure how much it is worth digging my heels in about anything. I used to think this had to do with my own set of insecurities, but increasingly, I think it is part of how closeness works. Sometimes, we have to forget or release a little about ourselves in order to connect to another person.

There are also times when this is too much to ask, when a child's sense that they cannot sustain an authentic self at school might be damaging. This is particularly true when differences between children and their teachers map onto institutionalized forms of social oppression: BIPOC children with white teachers, neurodivergent children with neurotypical teachers. Adults could make more space to remember what we are asking of children and consider the parts of themselves they sacrifice when they form close relationships with teachers.

## Being Yourself in a Group

My interviews showed me again and again that when children think of good relationships at school, they actually tend to think more about classmates and friends than teachers. For decades, psychologists have pointed out flaws in the culturally dominant narrative about peer relations becoming central only in adolescence. Yet for some reason, it remains easy for elementary practitioners to forget how important peer camaraderie is, even in first grade. Children are figuring out not only how to hold onto themselves while winning the admiration of their teachers, but also how they can work out a version of themselves in relation to a complicated social world.

My interview with Teenie, also from Ainsley's class, offers one of many examples of how much first graders might focus on peer relationships. Teenie and I had a long conversation about her relationship with her teacher. She told me how much she loves her teacher, how much she loved her kindergarten teacher too, and how much she loves all of the different grownups that work at her school. Then I asked Teenie, who does she feel close to at school? Since Teenie was one of the first children I interviewed, I thought the context of so much conversation about adults would lead her to mention one of them. She did not. Right away, Teenie answered, "Lyuba. She's my best friend and we're like we're sisters."

I asked Teenie why she feels so close to Lyuba, and she told me about a club she and Lyuba have. "It's called the Cheddar Girls and it's because we do it on the bus," she explained (Figure 1.1).

"We like… see me and Lyuba, we kind of go to a daycare after school because our parents need more time to work. So like,

**FIGURE 1.1** Teenie feels especially close to the Cheddar Girls when they are singing together on the bus.

we wear the same dresses, we go to the same daycare, and we sing a song, we sing about the Cheddar Girls and we just LOVE to be our club." Teenie told me more things about the Cheddar Girls. She explained, "We have to let other kids come in at school because there's no leaving out, so we have a different Cheddar Girls at school. That more kids are in it, so no one is left out."

I clarified, "But the original Cheddar Girls…"

"Oh yeah," she said, "That's just me and Lyuba. See, we like cheese a lot," she explained, "And Andrea, she doesn't even like it, she thinks it's the worst thing in the WORLD! And she doesn't like Sprite neither!"

Teenie's story shows a lot about closeness and how exciting it can feel to have a deep connection with a friend. For Teenie, so much of this is about having things in common and the wonders of liking the same thing as another person. Take a moment to think about this experience at the age of six. There is something you have had at home, called cheese. You know you like it, you know your family members like it too. Then, you use your growing capacity for language and overall self-expression to share that with another person – someone who you already think is pretty fun to be around – and you find out, they like this thing called cheese as much as you do! It is hard to overstate how joyful and even incredible that discovery can be for a child.

Just as incredible is the possibility that someone else could *know* about cheese and feel completely different about it. Teenie is scandalized by Andrea's difference, and it is this difference that means Andrea does not belong in the original club, only the fake one Teenie and Lyuba have cleverly devised to get around the school's regulations about exclusion. In a separate interview, Andrea also mentioned the Cheddar Girls, but in passing: "Sometimes I do the Cheddar Girls but I more rather play with Emmy," she said. As good as it feels to be *in* a close relationship like Teenie and Lyuba's, there is both struggle and strength in figuring out what it means to be *out*, figuring out what *you* "more rather."

Three times more children answered my question about closeness in school with elaborate descriptions of peer relationships than spoke about relationships with teachers. This surprised me, happening even as I contextualized my questions with the fact that I was investigating relationships between children and their teachers, and even as I previewed different ways that they do and do not feel close to their teachers. Children kept moving my project away from its starting point!

The complexity but also significance of the social worlds of childhood have so much to remind us about how children structure and contemplate relationships in general. In Teenie's case, there is also a story about figuring out herself and who she is in connection with closeness. Teenie connects to Lyuba for a lot of reasons, but most of them have to do with key attributes Teenie is identifying in herself. Andrea is a little different – she does not even like cheese! – and Teenie seems to wonder, what does this mean about how much I can let her in? Is she one of us? Can I be close to her?

After more discussion of the Cheddar Girls and their rituals, I asked Teenie again about her teachers. I asked, "Do you feel like you are close to Ms. Robyns?" Teenie responded, "I do feel close to my teacher Ms. Robyns. I do feel close to my teacher because our favorite color is the same color, it is pink." For Teenie, it feels important to share something with another person. These commonalities: a favorite color, an affinity for dairy – it is so easy to dismiss them as superficial in contrast to broader societal conversations about sameness and difference. Sharing a favorite color is nowhere near the same as sharing a racial identity, a religious belief system, or a worldview. Still, in childhood – and this came up in my interviews again and again – these things are terribly important, definitional, and part of what can feel like an overwhelming but exciting menu of options to choose from on the long path of figuring out who we are in the world.

After I spoke with Teenie, I had a chance to ask Ainsley what she thought about the Cheddar Girls. I wondered if she found the club intriguing or problematically exclusive. To my surprise, since Ainsley is the kind of teacher who generally has her finger on the pulse of what is going on with her students, she had never heard of the group. "I'll have to check that out," she mused. For me, this was a reminder of how complicated and important the secret social world of young children is, how when a teacher is busy forming strong relationships with children, the children's focus is sometimes much more intent on the society of one another, the society adults have nothing to do with.

## What About Teachers Holding onto Themselves?

In Laila and Benjamin's fifth grade class, difference is a frequent and overt topic of discussion. By fifth grade, most of the students at their school are well versed in a mentality that emphasizes appreciation of difference. In observations, it was much rarer than in Ainsley's class for all of the students to be working on the same thing at the same time. But the importance of emphasizing parts of the self that are shared with the teacher still came up frequently in interviews. Tanner, a quiet boy whose answers were mainly quite short, told me, "I like my teachers nicer when they like math a lot. Because I like math, you know." Aleah, one of the most outspoken girls in the class, described her friends, "I think we're close because… well, we laugh together, we like the same movies, same music… stuff like that." Then she added, "Ms. Audrey [Laila] likes the music too, did you know she likes Taylor Swift and musicals too?"

Thinking about ways a child can be incredibly different from their teacher in this much more racially and socioeconomically diverse class, I wondered how mandates for relationship building affect a child's sense of themselves. Is it possible for a child to feel close to a teacher with a different favorite color, or different taste in music, but still keep their own original favorite? I think it is, but the more central something feels to our identity, the harder it is going to be. What does a child do with themselves when they want to be close to their teacher, and their teacher wants to be close to them, but there is a need for compromise between them that cannot and should not be overlooked?

When a child acts like Jordan at the beginning of this chapter, asserting some bit of himself that does not fit into Ainsley's vision of her classroom, we sometimes decide the child's behavior is oppositional or otherwise problematic. We can relax this judgment, though, if we acknowledge some uncertainty. Are you truly sure that you can be close to someone else without losing track of central pillars of your selfhood? And are you sure that one of those things (individuality or closeness) matters as much as, or more than, the other?

I think a better answer to the question posed in this chapter is not yes or no, but "sometimes." If teachers felt a little less pressure to perform as if we knew a single right answer about navigating identity, individuality, connection, and separation all the time, we might find more generosity and joy in the playfulness children can so often bring to these boundaries. To do this, we have to stop posing "good relationships" as rules to abide by and acknowledge that they are only sometimes going to be children's priority, and even then, they are only sometimes going to work.

When I spoke with Laila and Benjamin about their teaching relationship, I got insight into their personal struggles with selfhood as it relates to closeness. Whenever I observed in their classroom, I admired how much their students saw both of them as central teacher figures, rather than one subsidiary to the other. To be sure, students relate to Laila and Benjamin differently. Among other things, many children seem to sort them into stereotypical, old-fashioned gender slots. They giggle more with Laila, and they work harder with Benjamin. They go to Laila with problems: arguments in friend groups, paper cuts that sting, chaotic mornings at home. With Benjamin, their conversations tend to be academic: "Why can't I remember $7 \times 8$? Look how long my paragraph is!" Having both teachers present in the classroom all the time offers a fantastic window into how savvy children are about figuring out what kind of adult is available for exactly what kind of relationship.

Benjamin and Laila's productive teaching relationship started to feel more complicated when I spoke with them during interviews. In one interview, when they were together, Benjamin expressed great confidence in his teaching philosophy. When I asked what kinds of values underlie his teaching, he answered right away, "Discipline, structure, consistency. I like to have a safe space, promoting excellence and high achievement, having high standards." Laila agreed that a safe space is important to her, but felt less confident in her answer. "That is my main goal…," she said, before trailing off. Then she continued, "I don't know. I'm still figuring it out. I still feel very brand new."

On a different day, I spoke with Laila alone. Benjamin was out sick, and I asked Laila about differences between her approach to relationships with students, and Benjamin's. "We're very different, we're really different in this category," Laila said immediately, and then went on to criticize herself, "I feel like I need to work on depersonalizing and I need to work on the separation… I definitely need to work on it." By "it," Laila meant being more like Benjamin in establishing firm emotional boundaries. It seemed to me that Laila's way of relating was benefiting the children, though, and Benjamin agreed when I followed up with him later, reflecting, "She doesn't have to be like me, what works for me [with kids] might not necessarily work for her… but sometimes, she thinks she needs to be like me. And she gets away from herself."

It is this getting away from the self that I wondered about so much with Laila and Benjamin, and then in turn with children in relation to their teachers. When a relationship functions well – and Laila and Benjamin's relationship does – can it mean that one person has folded in enough of the other to prevent a serious clash? In Laila's case, the cost is a lingering self-doubt. "Benjamin is really good at that," she frequently told me. "Benjamin really knows what he's doing in that area. I'm so lucky to work with him."

Built into many ideals of a relationship between teacher and child is a similar kind of admiration to what Laila expresses about

Benjamin. Don't we *want* kids to aspire to be more like their teachers? To read like them, complete math problems like them, engage as they do in conflict resolution? In school, we are asking children to let go of or look down on things about their current selves – their relatively low-level literacy, their inability to remember 7 × 8 – as they give in to the admiration that enables teaching and learning. But what happens to other things about themselves – their love of musicals, of the color pink, of cheese – if they do not fit with what the teacher seems to embody? Can a child be close to a teacher and still feel like they, the child, are good enough?

When I talked to Laila and Benjamin's students about them, what came up again and again was not the specialness of their relationship and mutual capacities, but the ways they are different from one another. Their fifth graders were determined to tell me about these differences, as if the fact of their teachers being distinct individuals was something I was at risk of missing, and it was their jobs to make sure I understood how important their differences were.

Jermaine, a small, quiet boy who rarely spoke up in class without it being demanded of him, told me, "Ms. Audrey [Laila] is, like, always nice and funny. Mr. Thatch [Benjamin] is more serious, strict and serious, but he can be nice, too." Sonja, a cheerful girl with a booming voice, said, "Mr. Thatch is really good at helping me with math. Ms. Audrey is better at helping me with reading, when I need help with the reading stuff." Emma, Sonja's more understated friend, said directly, "I really like both my teachers, but they are so so so so different to each other." Student after student, responding to any number of unrelated questions, emphasized differences between their two teachers: in personality, in strengths, in style of dress and tone of voice. It was as though the capacity of two such different people to coexist in a classroom was actually the main pedagogical outcome of the co-teaching relationship.

There are many reasons why children might be fascinated by the ways their teachers are different from one another. One reason may be that these children are interested in whether it is possible for two people to hold onto themselves as distinct individuals while still working well in concert. The answer is not simple, and the example before them is not a straightforward one. Both Laila and Benjamin feel that sometimes Laila gets lost in the dynamics of their collaboration. Children are looking not just at their two different teachers as models, but at the relationship between their teachers as one of life's examples of how a relationship can unfold, and what becomes of one person when they are put into close and constant conversation with another.

## Closing with Questions

I am not sure why we feel like we need to pretend, in teaching, that there are very clear boundaries between people or that humans have a solid understanding of coexistence amid big and small differences, all while asking teachers and students to form and sustain strong relationships with one another. It is actually not always so easy to understand where one person ends and another begins, and that slipperiness does not have to be scary or avoided. At the same time, teachers can try to tune in to moments when children are asserting core aspects of themselves, even as we reckon with the challenges these aspects pose. We have to do a better job acknowledging that we – teachers, adults – are unsure how much of ourselves we sometimes give up as we forge relationships with others. Similarly, we can admit that it is really hard to genuinely let another person flourish in their very different self. Sometimes, that other person – for a moment or much longer – is a bear.

Here are some questions for you to consider, allowing for uncertainty, as you reflect on the themes in this chapter:

- ♦ What are some of the times in your classroom that you feel strong in your own beliefs and identity?

*Think about the conditions that color your answer to this question. Does it depend more on things happening for you outside, or in the classroom? What aspects of your beliefs and identity come most firmly to mind, and why do you think this is true for you? How is the "self" you bring to teaching like and unlike the "self" you bring to other relationships?*

- During your teaching day do you notice children feeling especially strong about who they are? What kind of effect does that have on you?

   *In your answer to this question, are you thinking more about things children say, or ways they behave? What happens in your classroom when children are showing something about themselves that makes your teaching more difficult or might be making the day more difficult for other children?*

- Who do you think your own students consider their closest relationships to be with, and why? What does that make you think about being their teacher?

   *Keeping in mind what Teenie and Ainsley said about the Cheddar Girls, how much do you feel like you understand your students' social relationships with one another or other children? What reaction do you have to the possibility that children might feel closer to one another than they do to you as a teacher? How seriously do you take the social relationships among your students?*

- What are some times when it has been harder or easier for you to hold onto yourself in close relationships with others?

   *Simply reflect on what it means to you to keep a sense of yourself while still being close to another person, even when they are really different from you. How important does that feel to you? How do you think your beliefs in this area do or don't impact your teaching and what you expect from your students behaviorally and relationally?*

# 2

# Can You Be Close to Someone Who Has Power Over You?

Teachers have a lot of power over students. We can punish them, turn their day from bad to good or vice versa, make their parents proud, or get them into trouble at home. This is an unusual set of capacities in a socially valued relationship. On the other hand, many relationships operate with some sort of power differential, even if ideas about where "more" of the power lies fluctuate over time and across circumstances. In teaching, there are plenty of times when it appears as though students have the most power. I am often struck, discussing challenging issues in classroom management with teachers, by how many difficult emotional moments in teaching grow from a teacher's sense of their students' excess power over them.

    This chapter explores what happens in classroom relationships when power dynamics come to the fore. What do teachers think about their own power? How do students experience the power teachers hold, and how might this impact their sense of the relationship? When we ask teachers to develop strong relationships with children, are we asking for them to be less than honest about the extent of their power? Can a child really be close to someone who has power over them? To explore these questions, we should continue to work on thinking about classroom interactions from the child's standpoint, even while understanding the impossibility of fully accessing their perspective.

Children will also experience power in classrooms differently from one another, and this will certainly affect their interest in entering into a relationship with their teacher. Do they *have to* be part of this relationship? When a teacher works hard to form a relationship with a child, is it just that – hard and important work – or is it something more aggressive, pushing intimacy on someone who may not be interested? We will examine how some issues around power play out in Ainsley, Laila, and Benjamin's classrooms, and I will encourage you to think with me about power and relationships in your own practice.

## Love, Power, and "Teacher Mode"

Ainsley actually thinks a lot about her power over her students. She brought this up many different times in our interviews. Particularly, Ainsley described the importance of "getting out of teacher mode" as a way of promoting closeness. "As a teacher," she described, "it's so easy to divert our energy to the million other things that need to get done, and use the power we have to dismiss the students and the things they really need from us. Dismiss their vulnerability." When students come to her with problems, she tries to "be the best friend I can be, and get out of 'teacher mode' [she gestured with air quotes]… a friend will sit with you, listen, and remind you that you are loved." For Ainsley, showing students the right amount of love means relinquishing some of her power in moments of particular vulnerability.

I asked Ainsley to say more about what it means to release the power of "teacher mode." She responded, "Well, young children are surrounded by adults telling them what to do and how to do it. Sometimes all they are craving is a true friend." Ainsley believes that when the power in the student/teacher relationship is most prevalent and evident, the relationship is most likely to go awry. She described something a former professor told her.

> He gave me this advice. When you're talking down to children, they feel intimidated. They know you're talking down to them. If you want them to really hear what you're saying, you want to get on their level. So I always have it in the back of my head that if I want them to really hear me, then I need them to really see my face. If I want them to know that I'm really caring or sympathizing with them, they feel it so much more, they see my brow furrow… and it's like, I'm on your team, we're huddling right now.

Ainsley knows, though, that sometimes "teacher mode" is where she needs to be, and if she steps out of it for too long, she worries. "I worry about time," she said, "because sometimes my students want to tell me their entire life story. And you'd think that would be kind of short for a six-year-old, but it's not! And there just isn't enough time to listen." She lamented, "These are the times I find myself getting really strict, when my students want to laugh, be silly, and play with me, and I am on a strict time schedule to teach them."

A lot of teachers can probably relate to this sense that the demands of teaching get in the way of the same relationships we are told constantly to cultivate. It is hard to identify an appropriate line between being there as friend to a child and establishing boundaries that allow us to accomplish the many tasks we are meant to fit into a day. After all, being in "teacher mode" could also be called doing our job.

I asked Ainsley more about how she handles it when she notices time getting in the way like this, and she responded,

> Usually, that's when I get annoyed, and I tell them, I tell them I'm annoyed, and then it's back there, 'teacher

mode'... and they do still know I love them underneath it but it gets different when that happens. Like, okay, we were having fun, we were being friends, but now I need us to focus on blending sounds. And that *is* my job, and they know that, but it's different.

This is a pretty comprehensive description of how relationships can work in teaching. A teacher and a child might be close, but there is also a limit – a necessary one – because of curriculum, time, and the nature of their roles in relation to one another. That is inevitable, but it is also at an extreme point right now in high-poverty, high-control schools like Ainsley's. The curriculum requirements are incredibly rigid, and teachers feel the crunch of time so tightly. Of course this affects a sense of closeness in the classroom, because when teachers feel anxious about all the forces that have power over them, they often turn a less forgiving version of power onto their students.

Power differentials between teachers and students affect their capacities for closeness in other ways, too. A white teacher often has an unspoken level of racist, racialized power over students of color, and an English-speaking teacher has compounded linguistic and cultural power over students with other primary languages. In wealthy districts, when most students' families have more capital than teachers, power dynamics look different from those in the districts where Ainsley, Laila, and Benjamin work, where teachers often have more economic resources than the students and families they serve. Any time intersectional identity issues come into play, there is an ethical quandary about requesting a relationship. Why should a child be willing to expose themselves to the additional vulnerability necessary to form and sustain a relationship with their teacher?

I sometimes wondered if Ainsley's description of stepping out of "teacher mode" was a little disingenuous. A child can feel intense love for their teacher, but on some level, most children are still aware that the teacher is by definition an authority figure who has a lot of power over them. Is it better to acknowledge the consistency of that power more openly, similar to the importance of acknowledging systemic or institutionalized power in other domains as part of a move toward justice? Or does Ainsley have the right idea that it means more to children to try as hard and often as we can to step outside of that unequal gradient?

## Wanting to Impress

Children in both classes were aware of their teachers' power over them. One way that this consistently came through was in their articulation of how much they wanted to impress their teachers. They spoke so much about wanting to get things right and worried tremendously about getting things wrong. Colin, a student in Laila and Benjamin's class, was particularly direct. "I get angry when I get it wrong," he said, "like when I get a math thing wrong, or a spelling thing... I get angry because when you get stuff wrong, Ms. Audrey usually says, 'It's okay, you get some things right, you get some things wrong,' but I can tell she doesn't like it." I asked Colin how it feels when Ms. Audrey "doesn't like it," and he answered, "like she's mad at me but she doesn't want to tell me."

Students in both classes described relationships with their teachers in this way: a sort of contingent mutual care that could be easily disrupted by getting something wrong. Josie, in Ainsley's class, worried that sometimes she feels confused by her teacher. She told me that her mom told her she blinks a lot when she gets confused. "And *that's* what it said on my report card, that I blink a lot if I don't understand!" She seemed affronted that this was the impression she made on her teacher, and that Ainsley would go as far as putting it in a report. Carissa, another first grader, explained that "you know you feel close to someone if they like you and if they say nice things about you."

Zed, in the same class as Josie, also connected closeness with Ainsley to impressing or pleasing her in some way, or getting a good report. I asked him if he feels close to her and he answered,

"No, not really. I'm not close to teachers." Then I asked how he can tell if a teacher cares about him, and he said, "Just if they say nice things about you!" I asked him what kinds of nice things Ainsley might say about him, and he thought for a while, "My teachers do kind of care about me but I don't know why." He paused and grinned. "But sometimes I can be kind of a HANDFUL," he said, sounding proud but also relating this to his overall confusion about why his teacher might care about him. He paused again. "But my little baby sister? She can walk and run and REALLY be a handful." As I thought about what to ask Zed next, he decided to continue by reminding me of how closeness to a friend can sometimes feel better, and maybe less conditional, than closeness to a teacher. "The teachers," he said, "it just all depends, but I think that's fine. My friend Owen is the one who ALWAYS makes me laugh."

Wanting to impress a teacher is often an unnamed but incredibly important part of how education works. I have learned the most and accomplished my most difficult, complex, and careful work when I have had a teacher to show off for, when I felt as though their care for me was related to how well I did and how hard I worked. For many people, this is a sensible and adaptive dynamic. We project our own desires for growth and engagement onto a teacher or coach as a way to motivate ourselves, and it helps us achieve things. But the same dynamic can also disrupt closeness, and when it goes unspoken, a child may feel confused. Zed's story, where he ends up shrugging off the possibility of closeness with Ainsley by elevating his relationship with his friend, is another significant reminder of how meaningful peer relationships can be to children. It is also sort of a story of how a child who feels like he cannot meet his teacher's expectations might protect himself by just deciding to feel less connected to his teacher. If something feels unattainable, why pursue it?

Ainsley is devoted to naming her love for her students as though it has no contingency, and I think this is how truly she experiences it. But for Zed, and some of the other "handfuls" in her class, the power she has over their days and their sense of themselves is palpable. Again, it's not that there is something wrong with turning elsewhere when one relationship causes undue insecurity. It's just, there is something worth naming here about the ways power influences closeness. It would be a mistake to imagine that children are not, from a very young age, aware of this dynamic.

## Power, "Work Relationships," and Closeness

When I joined the department where I currently teach, I made friends with another new hire. We learned the ropes together. Since she was from the area, she was helpful in orienting me. We were guarded with our impressions of the job for the first semester or so; for me, this was mainly because of anxieties around proving myself and staking a claim in my work. But this eased after a few months, and we started spending more time together at the office, laughing and figuring things out. Our relationship rarely moved outside of work, except for occasional short texts, but for a work relationship, it felt like a close one.

Then, the chair of our department decided to step down, and my friend was the next logical one in line for the position. I felt incredible gratitude that she was willing to take it on. She became chair, and this means that now she has a sort of power over me. She writes my recommendations for promotion, runs department meetings, and has final say on various departmental issues.

The funny thing is, I anticipated that this would change our relationship more than it did. For a while, I stopped texting her casually, unsure whether that was even appropriate. Then things kind of bounced back. We still laugh together, share low-key stories about our families, talk through complicated issues on campus. I still think of her as a friend. But the power dynamic is also real. It came up when she observed my classes last fall, and I found myself significantly more nervous than I had been when my previous chair did teaching evaluations. It's harder to be evaluated by a friend! Like the children I interviewed, I wanted to not just get a good evaluation, but to impress her personally.

Still, overall, our closeness was not impacted much by the new power dynamic between us. I found this pleasantly surprising, like evidence that power does not necessarily have that much impact on a relationship. As I thought about it more, though, I realized it was because of the unspoken boundaries our relationship already had that the power dynamic was not destructive. We are close – but we are "work friends." I think this is similar to the relationship a lot of children have with their teachers, and sometimes it is equal parts boundary and relationship that allows for flourishing.

In my relationships with different kinds of boundaries, power gets in the way a lot more. My relationships with my two children are some of the closest, most meaningful relationships in my life: loving, ever-evolving, and strong. But I do have power over my children, and when I wield it in anger, frustration, sloppiness, or dismay, I see the profound impact it has on their sense of themselves. This is, to an extent, what it is to be a parent, and it is both analogous to and much more tangled than the ways a teacher uses their power.

I have felt my children distance themselves from me – turn to friends, to my wife, to one another – at times when my power feels too evident or painful. This can hurt, but it can also help them figure things out, live more full and honest lives as independent selves. I can't impose an idealized vision of what our relationships look like onto how they actually are, or else I get in the way of them figuring out the story from their points of view. Similarly, for many children, it is not going to be up to teachers to declare, "We have good relationships." The real story is more changeable, unequal, uncertain, and complicated than that.

## Closeness, Power, and Bodies in the Classroom

One of the ways I thought about power in both classrooms had to do with the teachers' physical presence, and particularly the use of touch, in relation to students. Ainsley is a very physical teacher. She bends down to students' height, looks them right in the eye, and puts her hands on their shoulders to guide, settle, or redirect them. She always asks students before hugging them, but she does this a lot, and students come to her for hugs frequently. For Ainsley, this is part of how she connects with children. She described, "Young children… not all of them, but for some of them, that touch is how they get a sense of connection. A lot of them like to hug me, run up to me, throw their arms around me, ask for a hug. I'm always ready with a hug when a child wants one."

There can be a lot of taboo about touch between teachers and children, but when I saw how it worked in Ainsley's class, it mainly felt like an extension or illustration of her constant telling them how much she loves them, how important they are. I also wondered about the power dynamic of touch: Does a child feel they can say no to a teacher who is offering a hug? What about the size difference between a teacher and a seven-year-old, when the teacher looms physically close?

Laila and Benjamin have a completely different approach to touch in their classroom. During observations, I saw frequent verbal redirection but almost no physical touch. Occasionally, Laila put her hands on a student's shoulder to settle them. I never saw hugs, and in general the classroom had more of an air of physical distance, everyone keeping to themselves. When I asked about it, Laila said, "There are definitely students who seek it, who come in and say, I need a hug, and I try to provide it. Or if they get overstimulated and a back rub would calm them down. But I definitely don't actively consciously go out and hug a student if they don't come to me."

Benjamin has stronger views about physical touch between a teacher and a student. He described a previous job at a school for students who were convicted sex offenders,

> I was immersed in 'Don't touch, don't go near.' I was conditioned to not cross that line... and then I worked at a middle school, which was very much hands to yourself. And then there's a stigma with being a male... I have learned to keep my distance. They ask for a hug and I tell them no, how about a high five. It makes me feel uncomfortable.

I understand what Laila and Benjamin mean about the importance of physical boundaries with children, and obviously fifth graders and first graders often inhabit their bodies quite differently at school. What is the right amount for teachers to be physical with their students, or to maintain a physical boundary? This is a place where uncertainty is key; any definitive answer feels wrong from another perspective. Sometimes, Ainsley's use of touch with her students seems incredibly loving, like something that facilitates connection. Other times, perhaps it is too much: a way of unconsciously exerting power and showing children how small they are, how little is under their control. The same, though, is true of Laila and Benjamin's physical distance. On the one hand, it is appropriate, professional boundary-setting that enables kids to separate and enjoy bodily autonomy. On the other hand, the decision to withhold touch is still very much an adult decision, and the anxiety about what touch might mean is an adult anxiety.

The uncertain and ever-changing rules, norms, and feelings teachers face and experience about touch in the classroom show how much of the child's experience of the relationship with their teacher is in the teacher's power. Teachers and students exist in relation to one another, but from the point of view of children, the rules of engagement are in the teacher's hands. There are other professional relationships – medical interactions come to mind – where one of the parties makes so many of the physical decisions. Is genuine closeness possible in the face of this kind of unequal power distribution? Can you be close to someone who decides when and whether touch is okay, even deciding on your behalf whether or not you need it?

## They're Mean When They Yell at You and Tell You What to Do

*It is December, and Ainsley has been reading her students books about winter holidays. She has just finished a Hanukkah picture book that features an old lady, a goblin, and a little boy who teaches them the wonder of the holiday. Ainsley asks her students what they thought about the book, and Conrad gingerly raises his hand, "That old lady was mean."*

*Several other kids nod, and Ainsley asks, "What makes a person mean?" She is trying to get the children to think about what kinds of feelings might lead a person to engage in mean behavior, but they interpret the question as "what makes you say she is mean?"*

*Conrad continues, "She's mean because she's just a grouchy old lady. She yells at the kids and she says, do this, do that!"*

*Ainsley asks, "But isn't that what grownups do sometimes, to try to help children? Like I might say, Conrad, go get your jacket on for recess, Conrad, tie your shoes."*

*"Yeah," Simone interjects, "But that's not mean for you to do that."*

*Ainsley smiles and asks, "What do you think the difference is?"*

*Conrad answers her, "The difference is, they're mean. They're mean when they yell at you and tell you what to do." Several other children nod, and the class overall seems to think the matter is settled.*

In this conversation, Ainsley pushes on Conrad and the others to get more deeply at their thoughts about authority, and it was hard for the children. When you believe that grownups have your best interests at heart, it is difficult to pinpoint what there is to criticize about their "telling you what to do." But Conrad knows there is something regarding the woman in the picture book he does not like, and he is not quite ready to let Ainsley off the hook the way Simone does. On some level, he is sending Ainsley a message about how it feels when she gives him instructions. Some of the other students might be thinking about this too.

When I interviewed Conrad a few weeks later, he proved to be one of the many children much more interested in talking about his connections with other children than with his teacher. I asked, "Do you feel close with Mrs. Robyns?" He shrugged and said, "She's nice!" very enthusiastically. Then he went on, "But I'm going to be an astronaut. And Owen and Jack are going to be astronauts too. We're going to go to space." What a move of exerting autonomy – this is what I am going to be! – instead of succumbing to the power that he senses in his teacher.

Just as I wondered with Teenie and Lyuba in Chapter 1, I wondered again with Conrad, does he truly have to have a *relationship* with his teacher? Can we let him just get by in her class, or is he subject to a mandate to connect? Teachers face constant messages that having a good relationship with our students is part of what makes a good teacher, particularly as it relates to classroom management. But if a student is not that interested in the relationship, why should they have to partake?

## Power and Difference in Student/Teacher Relationships

Relationships between students and teachers also interact with a range of other socially mediated power dynamics besides age. Benjamin gestures toward this when he describes some of the specific stigma but also power associated with being a male elementary teacher; gender dynamics are incredibly real between students and teachers. White teachers also have often insufficiently named racialized power in relation to students of color. How could this not have an impact on a child's perception of the relationship?

All three teachers I worked with were white, which is certainly representative of the teaching corps in their region, and most of the paraprofessionals in both schools were BIPOC.

Already, then, students of all races are observing something in school about white adults in relatively powerful positions and BIPOC adults having less power. In all my time in schools, I have never heard adults address this systematized discrepancy directly with students.

In relationships between BIPOC students and white teachers, requests for compliance, directives, and attempts at closeness are always going to be mediated by racial difference. This does not mean wonderful things cannot happen within these relationships, but sometimes, real consideration of race and power makes a classroom interaction read differently from how it might initially look.

## Around the World

*Laila is working with Javier, Lily, Rosie, and Sam during math. They are reviewing different strategies for double-digit multiplication. Javier is Latino; the other three students in this group are white. Laila tries to move their attention to the next problem on the page.*

"Can we play a game instead?" *Javier asks.*

"Not today," *Laila answers,* "I want to finish these problems, and I want you to be good at it."

"But what if we play Around the World?" *Javier presses. This is a trivia game Laila and Benjamin often play with their students for review. It is fun and beloved but raucous and very competitive.*

"No," *says Laila,* "Come on, let's look at the worksheet. What strategy do you think you'll use for this next one, Rosie?"

*Rosie looks at her sheet for a moment and then back at Laila.* "I guess maybe open arrays…"

"That's right, Rosie!" *Laila sounds cheerful,* "Javier, can you use an open array for this one?" *Sam turns around in his seat and starts flicking dust from his pencil eraser onto the floor. Lily nudges him,* "Quit!" *but Laila doesn't seem to notice.* "Javier, I know you can, you can do it!"

"When can we play Around the World again?" *Javier asks,* "We didn't play it for a really long time!"

*"Come on, Javier,"* Laila says, sounding exasperated, *"I said no. I need you to be focused now."* At this point, Rosie is working on the problems further down on her worksheet, and Sam and Lily are poking each other back and forth with erasers. *"I know you can do it,"* Laila continues, making direct eye contact with Javier, *"I want you to be good at it. I want YOU to feel like you can do it."*

*"And then can we play Around the World?"* Javier persists.

*"No,"* Laila pronounces carefully, *"That game gives me stress. It gives me too much stress for the rest of the day, and I want you to feel like you can do this. Come on, Javier, let's get focused. Rosie, you've done a lot!"*

On the one hand, this is a companionable story of a small group of students working together, Laila trying to keep them on track. On the other hand, it is a story of the one brown child in a group of white people getting repeatedly shut down, and the low-grade shenanigans of two white children being overlooked. Laila is always relaxed and friendly with her students, and this vignette was no exception. Even her disinterest in acceding to Javier's wishes had a gentle undertone, with her continually coaxing him toward a sense of success with the math. Still, it stood out how much, how firmly and how confidently she said no to him. Teachers cannot say yes every time a child asks for a game or special activity! However, we can focus on who in our classroom we are saying "no" to, whose distractions do and do not get our attention and correction.

All three teachers dismissed the notion of any impact of race or ethnicity on their relationships with their students. "I try to find something in every single student that I share or connect with," Ainsley told me, "so even if our skin looks different, even if our home lives might sometimes look very different, there is always something we have in common." Laila framed the idea differently, "I just want them all to have a safe space, for the classroom to be a safe environment… that's important to me. I think it doesn't matter as much where they come from, what they look like. No matter what, it's my job to help kids feel safe when they are in school, and that is important to me."

These reactions surprised me, given how much public discourse most educators have encountered in recent years around, for example, internalized racism and unconscious bias. Perhaps Ainsley and Laila lacked insight into these concepts, or perhaps in order to function professionally, they needed to believe in their own capacities to move past or work without bias.

In the Around the World story, there is no indication that Javier or any of the children in the group feel unsafe. The tone is relaxed, and corrections are done in an understated, humorous way. Yet this idea that a child *has to* feel safe as a way of gratifying a teacher's sense of self, of good practice, asks more of BIPOC children with a white teacher than it does of their white peers. Javier, because of so many institutionalized dynamics around race and culture, has to take more risks to ask something of his teacher than Lily, Rosie, or Sam do. Hearing "no" means something different, and it is likely a lesson about power and relationship that he learns many times over the course of an ordinary day at school.

There is a temptation among many white people to disclaim the power that comes with our race, and perhaps among teachers in particular to prove that we can relate to our students "no matter what." It would be outrageous, and deeply problematic, for teachers to give up on relating to students because of racial differences. At the same time, are BIPOC children under some kind of obligation to indulge white teachers' fantasies about how un-racist we are by playing into a particular idea of a relationship? It feels unfair to require a relationship of Javier, along with all of the other things school already requires from him.

## Closing with Questions

Power dynamics, even power inequities, are not necessarily bad. But teaching without being sure means acknowledging that children will rarely be upfront, perhaps even with themselves but certainly with adults, about how much their observations of power in a classroom are impacting their relationships with the teacher. An edginess about admitting its absence is part of power's story, after all.

Again, I am left wondering if the language of "relationship" is sometimes ill-suited to describe what unfolds in a classroom. Maybe some (not all!) children would prefer an option to say: just teach me stuff, and let go of your attempts to KNOW me, to be close to me. We cannot pretend power is irrelevant in these interactions, or that anyone has a handle for sure on whether and what kind of closeness is possible in the face of a range of inequities.

The questions here are intended to help you apply some of the ideas in this chapter to your own teaching. Try to be as honest with yourself as you can, even about uncertainties, regarding power as it may play out in your relationships – especially with students.

- ♦ When have you felt close to someone who has power over you, or who you have power over? How do you imagine the other person experienced that relationship?

    *Often, power works in different ways within even one relationship. What about some times that you felt someone was exerting power over you – how did this impact your sense of closeness to that person? Think about how this relates to students' potential experiences of their relationships with you or other teachers.*

- ♦ What are some of the ways intersectional issues around power, like racial and socioeconomic identities, impact your relationships with your students?

    *Think about the ways you do and do not carry social privilege in relation to your students. Even young children are aware of these dynamics. How do they impact what you do and do not ask of your students? What happens when you think about your race, gender, sexual orientation, socioeconomic identity, or other intersectional issues through the eyes of different children in your class?*

- What do you notice about the differences between how the teachers in this chapter think about power in relationships and how their students do? What does that make you think or wonder about your own practice?

    *For example, reflect on the difference between Ainsley's use of touch in her classroom, and Laila and Benjamin's approach to physical relationships with children. Think about whom you feel more similar to and why, and how this impacts your students' perception of your power over them. Think, also, about the ways Laila, Benjamin, and Ainsley are and aren't aware of their own power as they interact with children, and reflect on what this makes you think or wonder about your own teaching practice.*

# 3

# Can You Be Close to Someone and Be Very Different from Them?

This chapter considers what happens to closeness in the face of the big and small differences that come up constantly in classrooms. There are seemingly minor differences, like someone's taste in food or sports. Then, there are more substantive differences, like race and gender.

The question of how similarities and differences impact closeness is related to what we considered in Chapter 1: whether being close to another person still allows you to hold onto yourself. Here, however, we will think more specifically about how differences impact both members of a relationship – not just whether a difference can cause a child to lose track of herself, but also how the difference leads her to see herself, the teacher, and the nature of connection in the face of variation. To get us started, consider this anecdote from Laila and Benjamin's fifth grade.

## Glitter Can Be Good or Bad

*It is the week leading up to Halloween, and the students are excited. Earlier this week they made sugar skulls, and the plan this afternoon is to paint them. When I get there, they are in small groups for reading, but their attention is largely on the white molded skulls lining the classroom.*

Laila has Edo, Eleanor, Honorah, and Sam in a small group. They are writing paragraphs in response to a reading comprehension question. It is an uphill battle. Edo, who is Latino, points at the wall, "When do we get to paint them?"

Laila answers, "This afternoon. For now let's keep working on our reading."

"Do we have to touch the glitter?" Edo asks.

Eleanor, a white girl, giggles. "How can you paint it if you don't touch it?"

"Guys," Laila interjects, "Come on, eyes on your papers."

"I don't like glitter either," Sam, a white boy, says quietly, looking over at Edo.

"Yeah same," Edo replies, "Same. I hate glitter."

"But these are so cute!" says Honorah, an Asian girl.

"GUYS!" Laila says a bit more loudly, and then she seems to relent, entering the kids' preferred conversation. "Come on, glitter is so fun! I love crafting, I really love working with glitter." Then she pauses and indicates their papers, "But don't forget, we can't even do it at all if you can't get your writing done."

"I HATE glitter," Sam states boldly. Edo laughs.

"Yeah, me too," says Edo. Laila leans over to Edo's page and points at it, trying hard to get him to keep writing. "NO GLITTER ALLOWED!" he yells.

"Hey!" says Eleanor, "I love glitter! And Honorah too, she has glitter on her nails!"

"I love glitter, it's so CRAFTY!" says Honorah. "Glitter is so, so good."

"It's good, it's good," Eleanor shouts.

Laila smiles, "Girls, I like glitter, too. And I love that you used that word crafty," she tells Honorah, "but we only have ten minutes to finish our paragraph."

"Glitter is STRESSFUL," Edo proclaims, and then repeats Sam's phrase, "No glitter allowed." Sam and Edo start to laugh loudly, and Edo accidentally knocks several open packets of baby carrots, left over from snack, onto the floor.

"EDO!" Laila sounds angry now, and I see Benjamin look up from the other side of the room.

"Edo," he says, walking over, having apparently heard the whole conversation, "People have different opinions. Glitter can be good or bad. But I need you to do your work, my friend, and if I have to ask you again, it won't be nice."

All four children, chastened, bend dutifully over their work for the remaining ten minutes.

Sometimes, children and teachers are secure in their own stances but still figuring out what it means to be in close contact with someone who either feels or is different. In this vignette, Edo and Sam team up along lines of sameness. Is it because they are both boys, or just because they both dislike working with glitter? Honorah and Eleanor also form a gentle alliance that, again, might be about gender or might be about an unrelated affinity. Laila seems ambivalent – she likes glitter too, and she wants the boys to share this with her, to be excited about the project, which she hopes includes plenty of glitter. Benjamin steps in with something a bit firmer and also affirms the difference: glitter can be good or bad. That is true, but if you're a person for whom glitter is good, what can you make of someone who is sure it's bad?

The question about whether it is possible to be close to someone different from you in a big or a little way is a substantial one in teaching. Children, by virtue of age, are inherently different from their teachers. Thrown into a society of same-age peers, many children will form their closest relationships along the lines of sameness with friends, and the teacher is a bit of an incidental character. Think of the adult voice in the Peanuts cartoons, "Wah wah wah," droning on; this same adult voice is the one teachers spend years crafting and tuning.

When a teacher makes themselves known to their class – lets the kids know, for instance, that they celebrate Halloween, that they play basketball or like glitter – some children do an internal calculus about what this piece of information means about their relationship to the teacher. When Laila determines that "glitter is fun," Edo and Sam have to figure out what that means about their relationship to her. It is one of those surprisingly fraught moments that happen all the time in the classroom because of the diversity that exists among human beings, and though there is no right or wrong way to address it, teachers need to spend more time thinking and talking about it.

We are missing something important if we do not attend to how children's findings in the ongoing investigations they make into sameness and difference impact classroom relationships. Staying alert to the ways societal constructs around difference interplay with momentary interactions in classrooms is crucial if we are thinking about fostering relationships in the face of difference. So, too, is taking seriously the gravity of differences, for many children, that adults might be inclined to dismiss as fleeting or superficial.

## Difference in Personal Relationships

What are some times that you have felt close to someone who was different from you? How has difference played out in your relationship? These answers are rarely simple. I have four sisters, and all of us love to read. With one of them, almost every time we talk, we share what we are reading; we share recommendations and sometimes get into bigger conversations about the books we have both read. We don't always love the same books, but our tastes are pretty aligned. We almost always gift each other books for holidays. In fact, sharing books is one of the most significant aspects of our relationship, and every time we talk about a book, we learn more about each other. The similarities of our affinities in this way exist because we are close, but they also bring us closer.

By contrast, another one of my sisters almost never likes the same books I do, and though I have tried a lot of her recommendations, I can rarely get through them. This seems like such a small thing when we have so much else in common, including shared history, other shared tastes and interests, and a mutual love for each other. But actually, it isn't small! It seems like it becomes a proxy for other differences between us too, and like a topic we have to actively avoid. I don't picture us ever getting into a fight over a book one of us liked and the other didn't. But there is this sense of anxiety or insecurity around the difference, as if by not liking the same things, one of us is somehow deeming the other "wrong."

For a long time, I assumed this anxiety was based in my own sense of insecurity or inferiority, but when I broach the topic with other people, many can relate. Being different from someone else – liking different pizza toppings, having different systems for loading a dishwasher, preferring one or another kind of music, responding differently to being in a big crowd – these are serious things to negotiate in a relationship partly because each of them is tied up with other things about ourselves, and partly because somebody else wanting to do things differently can so quickly feel like a negative judgment about our own desires, habits, and hopes. It becomes not just a question about holding onto our sense of self, but also a question about appreciating, if not understanding, other people we are in contact with.

We are so often naturally drawn to other people with whom we have things in common. But teachers and students frequently have very little in common, other than the space they occupy for six or so hours a day. This makes the ask for a relationship so complicated, though arguably also so beautiful. There are times when a child's relationship with their teacher might be the only relationship they ever have with someone with a certain set of characteristics.

Definitely my own teaching experiences are like that. When I taught elementary school, I had relationships with people who prioritized athletics above all else, people who spoke Portuguese at home, people who lived in homeless shelters, and one person whose family had a private airplane. I have never had other relationships with people with these characteristics or experiences, none of which I share. Now, in higher education, I have relationships with dozens of people who are first-generation college students – also different from me – with people who love to party, people whose dream vacations include sleeping outdoors. I adore this about teaching, that it brings me into contact with so many people who are different from myself and from each other, that I can learn to respect and admire these differences. At the same time, the differences clearly impact the relationship, and there is no denying a particular spark when I meet a student who shares something important with me.

So often, too, these shares are full of cultural and socioeconomic significance. "Oh, my dad is a college professor, too! Oh, I was also born when my mother was in medical school! I, too, love artichokes and traveling to Europe!" The anecdotes that follow zoom in on a few small moments of conflict between teacher and student that are simultaneously about little and big things.

## I Wouldn't Have Known You Were Joking

*Ainsley is bringing her students in from recess. When they get to the classroom, it is clear that Carissa, a white girl, is crying. Ainsley holds her hand and crouches down beside her. "We're going to talk this through," she tells Carissa. "Everyone else, I need you to take a seat and sit patiently."*

*Ainsley beckons for BJ, also white, to come stand with her and Carissa. "BJ," she says to him, while other students either sit down or cluster nearby, listening, "What did you tell Carissa?"*

*"I was only joking," BJ says.*

*"But what did you say?" Ainsley presses.*

*BJ whispers, "I said I was going to kill her. Not for real though!"*

*Ainsley drops Carissa's hand and uses both of her hands to cup BJ's face. "We do not joke like that," she says to BJ, "I know you think you were joking, but we don't joke like that. Carissa did not know you were joking. I wouldn't have known you were joking."*

*"I didn't say it TO her," BJ says, still whispering.*

*"Regardless," Ainsley pronounces slowly, "We don't say that. We don't want anyone in this school to feel unsafe."*

*BJ turns to Carissa and mutters, "Sorry."*

I understood why Ainsley needed to take a hard line on this episode, because Carissa was upset and even a joking death threat has such a serious undertone. The undertone is, of course, made more serious by a global and national context entirely outside of BJ's control, where school shootings and violence are considerable concerns.

Still, from the outside, it was hard not to sympathize with BJ a bit. He was pushed to the fringes of an alliance between Carissa and Ainsley, who both responded with the same upset and severity to something he says he meant as a joke. It is hard to know what his original intention was, of course – maybe he is just responding to being overwhelmed since his teacher is angry with him – but either way, he sees the initial incident really differently from how they did.

Ainsley ended the reprimand with a reminder that everyone needs to feel safe in school. But I don't think BJ felt that safe as this unfolded. His use of a whisper, his furtive glancing around, all indicated that he felt under a certain kind of threat. The thing about safety is that different things make different people feel safe. Because of that, it is oversimple to imagine "feeling safe in school" as something that can be handled via particular rules and procedures. Maybe it is something that cannot be handled at all.

The conflict unfolded because BJ and Carissa had different responses to the same set of words. For BJ, it could be a joke. Perhaps he jokes like this frequently with friends and other people he feels close to. For Carissa, it absolutely was not a joke. Maybe no one in her world jokes this way, and she felt genuinely scared.

My first instinct as a teacher probably would have been similar to Ainsley's, at the very least a performed indignation that something like a death threat could be funny. But then I think about the ways my friends and I also sometimes use exaggerated language – "I'm so tired I want to DIE," "I'll murder you if you tell anyone," and BJ's utterance doesn't seem that outrageous. The line between his intent – to joke around – and his impact – pushing Carissa to tears – is a confusing line, based so much on differences in temperament, experience, and style. Ainsley allies herself with Carissa when she tells BJ that wouldn't have seemed like a joke to her, either, and I wonder what this does to BJ's sense of his relationship to his teacher. How can a teacher make room for these kinds of differences and sustain relationships with students on all sides of them?

### She's on Her Computer All Day

*In Laila and Benjamin's class, there is a time for about half an hour before lunch called WIN, or What I Need. Often, special educators and therapists come in to work with children during WIN, and it is also a time that students get caught up on projects or go over material they need more time to master. It is also a time that many students play on their Chromebooks.*

*Today, Birdy, white, has thick earphones on and is glued to her screen, toggling back and forth between a math game and a writing project. Javier finishes a worksheet he has been doing and asks Laila, "Can I get Birdy to work on our science?" The two of them are partners for a science poster. Laila nods; she is preoccupied helping some other students with math but gestures to where Birdy is sitting. Javier walks over.*

*First, he stands in front of Birdy and waves at her. Not getting a response, he pokes her gently on the arm. She ignores him. Javier taps her once more, still to no avail. He wanders back over to Laila. "Um, Ms. Audrey? She's not… she's not waking up."*

Laila laughs. "Oh, Birdy," she says, getting up to help Javier. "I don't understand it. I can't stare at screens that long without going berserk! But that's how she is with that computer, you know?"

"Yeah," says Javier, grinning, "I don't get like that either. She's on her computer ALL DAY." Laila laughs again, and Javier joins her in the chuckle before Laila leans down and removes Birdy's headphones to tell her to shift gears.

This story felt like such a companionable moment between Laila and Javier, and as I had by then grown accustomed to seeing Javier lightly reprimanded and redirected, it was nice to witness a moment of alliance between him and his teacher. They both seemed to enjoy the friendly laughter.

The complexity, of course, was that the laughter came at Birdy's expense, and again around a general theme of difference. It is true that Birdy gravitates toward the screen at every possible opportunity and seems most comfortable in school when she is typing or playing games online. She is on the outskirts of the various social scenes in Laila and Benjamin's classroom, but she is quite skilled with technology. Javier not only pokes light fun at her affinity, but also makes a point of highlighting his difference from her – a difference that then aligns him with his teacher. It is a pleasant moment in Laila and Javier's relationship. It is also a moment that promotes the sense that sameness makes closeness more possible.

This episode marked one of the few times in my observations that closeness and similarity about something like habits or tastes did not align with sameness in race and gender. I caught much more frequent occurrences of boys discussing commonalities with Benjamin (going fishing on the weekend, loving pants with lots of pockets, preferring adventure books to realistic fiction) and girls with Ainsley and Laila (loving arts and crafts, getting annoyed by the assumption that girls always like pink – but still liking pink, preferring kittens to puppies). It was breathtaking how many of these shared experiences aligned with truly old-fashioned sets of gender stereotypes and deeply embedded norms.

It was also quite rare for me to document a story of student commonality with teachers where the racial identity of the two involved was different; in fact, the preceding episode with Javier was the only such that I noted. All of this makes me wonder about how superficial commonalities can stand as proxies – kind of unspoken, unacknowledged substitutes – for broader social ones, and how the relationship between sameness and closeness leads children who are less likely to share key identities with teachers to be situated differently when it comes to this much valued "relationship."

## She's Different to My Mom, But She Takes Care of Me

A poignantly explicit conversation with a child who was thinking about the ways similarity and difference impact closeness happened during my interview with first-grader Finley. When Finley and I sat on small chairs in the hallway outside of Ainsley's classroom, she told me many different details about her life outside of school. She kept leading the conversation back to things that were going on in her world. "After school," she told me, "I really like to go home. I like to feel my mommy with a baby inside her. It's a girl," she went on, "And her due is May 4."

I remarked that Finley must feel close to her mom. She nodded. "My brother's first, then there's his first baby brother, then Jackson, then me, and soon another one, so he gets to be a bigger biggest brother."

Finley went into some other description of her family, telling me which of her siblings like to do what with whom. I told her it sounded like she is a girl who cares about her family. "Yeah…," she said, twirling a piece of hair around her finger. Then she took a surprising turn. "I have a lot of bad dreams," she told me. "I have bad dreams but I mean, they are like creepy dreams."

I told Finley I understood how scary that can be, and she asked, "Do you have bad dreams too?"

"Oh, sure," I told her, noticing how she seemed to be seeking commonality. "I think most people do. What do you do when you have bad dreams?"

"Do most people do?" she asked me.

I told Finley I was pretty sure, and she said, "Well, I tell my mom but you see, she doesn't have them. She doesn't get bad dreams. Sometimes I tell my friends but they don't get that many bad dreams either." Suddenly it occurred to her I might not like this, and she hurried to explain, "I mean, they won't get that scared from mine, though, they're already in first grade."

Momentarily surprised by the idea of a mom who never has bad dreams, I asked Finley, "Do you ever tell Ms. Robyns if you had a bad dream?"

"Oh YEAH," she answered, "I do, she's always very nice. She always says, we love you, we take care of you, and then she does. She gets bad dreams too sometimes, like you." She nodded and then looked at me almost as though to reassure me about the situation, "So she gets them too, like you," she repeated.

I asked Finley whether she likes talking to her teacher about her dreams and she nodded, "Yeah, I really love my teacher. She's different to my mom, but she takes care of me."

This conversation was one child's sophisticated exploration of how different people operate internally and then communicate about their thoughts and feelings. Finley was open about the struggle of her bad dreams – even with me, who she only knows vaguely, she admitted to this vulnerability and even described how strange it feels to find herself alone in a group of people who claim never to have bad dreams. At the same time, she clearly found it a relief to learn that I, like her, was familiar with the experience, and it meant something to her that Ainsley had told her something similar. The sameness was a great comfort. She also knows that this sameness is not a necessary precursor to a relationship. She feels very close to her mom, even without having something like that in common. She is also thinking about what it means to be close to two adult women who are so "different to" each other, but similar in their love and willingness to care for her.

Finley's research into this topic does not strike me as particularly different from my own or maybe most adults' when we are open with ourselves. It can be confusing for all of us to encounter people whose vulnerabilities and struggles do not align with our own, and more confusing still when this is a person we love and feel loves us in return. Does the difference compromise our closeness? Not exactly, but it does do *something*, so when we encounter sameness, it is consoling and meaningful.

I think about my wife, the adult I feel closest to in the world, and how different our struggles and vulnerabilities are from one another's. Sometimes, that helps us feel closer. It is probably easier for her to comfort me in unrealistic hypochondria precisely because that is just not something she struggles with. But it can also be a wedge: I find myself thinking, HOW can you not be just seething with worry about this new freckle, this pain in my shoulder? Do you understand me at all? When I talk to friends who share the hypochondria, that is comforting, a kind of closeness that can only exist through commonality. Still, I know in a deep way that the difference with my wife brings its own kind of closeness. It comes particularly from the ways we have to work a little harder to understand one another. Difference can be a blockade against something, but it allows for something else. All of these things are called relationships, but each one seems so distinct.

Finley, who experiences closeness to Ainsley as related to similarity, is, like Ainsley, a white female. Ainsley also shares so many experiences and characteristics with her students because of her explicit decision to teach in the community where she grew up and where her family of origin still lives. She comes from a socioeconomic background similar to many of her students, and she knows many of the same people they know, goes the same places they go on weekends, and has the same microcultural touchpoints.

Ainsley believes this makes her a stronger teacher. "A lot of times," she tells me,

> I understand what they are going through just because this is where I grew up too, this is the same neighborhood I would roller skate in... and the problems aren't that different from when I was coming up, either. I have to be careful, "not to make assumptions because of that, but I think it makes me a better teacher. It's why I'm better in this job than my last one" (where she had less in common with her students).

For Ainsley, it is intuitive that certain kinds of commonalities with her students will make her a better teacher for them, and will enable stronger, closer relationships. There are all kinds of formal and informal efforts to get people in a variety of professions to return to work in the communities where they were raised – for just the kinds of reasons Ainsley articulates. What's complicated, though, is how rarely we name the assumption this incorporates about sameness being preferable to difference. If it is, what happens to the children who fit a different profile and therefore just don't form an easy relationship with the teacher?

### They're Not My Friends

Of the three teachers, Benjamin seemed least interested in finding things in common with students. "I don't think it's that important," he told me, "because I intentionally keep my relationships pretty superficial with kids. They're not my friends, they're not my own children."

I told him that I have noticed him in what seems like a strong rapport with children and wondered if he was overstating this stance of distance. "I know what you mean," he said, "But that's just because... they want to identify with you, find something in common, have that relationship... So I've gotten very good at pretending. Even with a kid you just can't stand... you have to pretend."

At first, I was put off by what seemed like the coldness in this statement. How can a teacher speak so uncaringly about children? As I thought more about what Benjamin said here, though, I started to find a refreshing honesty in it. Benjamin is describing teaching without being sure, which can sometimes mean faking a connection you might not actually feel. Is it really possible to like every single child, even those whose behavior is so outside of your own frameworks and value systems that you "can't stand" them? Maybe, but also maybe not. When it feels impossible, pretending is one way through. It puts less pressure on a relationship than forcing the liking.

On the other hand, the total dismissal of the possibility of liking a child is hard to embrace. I want to lean into the idea that Ainsley describes: that every child has loveable attributes and that it is the teacher's job to find and respond to them. I wonder, though, if I want this idea so badly because of my own human desire for love and acceptance, even from people very different from me, people who might initially find me off-putting. Maybe distinct approaches to these questions just work for different teachers, and this is one of the many kinds of difference we have to deal with when thinking about schools.

### Finley's Different World

A few weeks after that conversation with Benjamin, I was back in Ainsley's classroom. My plan that day was observations, but Finley quickly approached. "Are you going to ask me more questions? Are you going to take me in the hall?"

Ainsley walked over and told Finley not to bother me, but I gestured for her not to worry. I asked Finley if she wanted to talk to me, and she thought for a moment. "Did I tell you," she wondered, "how my mom's landlord thinks that she lied to him?" I shook my head. "Well, she did not. She did not lie. But now I don't know where we're going to go."

I asked, "Oh, you need a new place to live?"

Finley nodded. We were standing awkwardly in an aisle between rows of desks, and most of the other children were either working on Chromebooks or in small groups with one of the teachers. Finley kept going, so badly did she want or need this moment of connection. "I don't know where we're going to go," she continued, "My teacher doesn't know yet, but I'll still be coming to this school." Everything about our interaction felt urgent. "I'm going to be at my grandma's for today," she told me, "but the thing is... it's turning into something really sad."

"That does sound so sad!" I agreed.

Finley went on, "My cats are really sad, and... all the minutes I think about going home and packing my room and I mean, it's fun to pack but I'm really sad that we are leaving."

I repeated, "It does sound really sad." It did feel sad, thinking about this child making her way through phonics exercises and addition and subtraction drills all while worrying, like so many children in the United States, about where she might sleep tonight. I was drawn to the world she painted, incredibly different from mine, because of her willingness to be vulnerable. I thought about how we might make more space for conversations like these, so important for the children who want them, so ill aligned with the demands of school.

"I did it before," Finley said, drawing up her body as though indicating a sense of strength, "I used to live at a small little blue house. My mom and my dad, they got in too many fights there so they broke up and... I mean, it's hard to get into a new happy life but then go into a sad life but we just have to, we have to go." Here, I noticed my internal reaction shifting. I, too, grew up with parents who "got in too many fights" and divorced, and even though everything else Finley described was unlike my experience, I noted a shift from a stance of admiration mixed with sympathy, to one of my own vulnerability and empathy. I wondered if the first reaction was actually more similar than I cared to admit to Benjamin's "pretending" – sure, I hear how sad that sounds! – whereas my reaction now seemed closer to intimacy. "I know just how hard that is." Did that shared thread bring us a bit closer?

Everything about what Finley shared was deeply moving to me. Maybe it was because we had a previous conversation about the concept of closeness, or maybe all of these things were so prevalent in her mind that when an outsider came in, she identified a good outlet. As so often happens when children share details from their out-of-school worlds, I was struck by both the gravity of what she had going on, and the sophistication she was bringing to bear in processing it. Even sharing her story here, I am suspicious of my motives: maybe I just want you, as a reader, to catch your breath as I did in recognition of the heavy weight so many children have to bear, at how hard they have to work to make sense of life circumstances that feel out of their control. Children so often have sad, complicated events in their lives, ones that might be unfathomable to many teachers. Does sympathizing with them bring us closer? Does proceeding with academics as planned? What does it do to our relationships when children sense that they are having to exert a level of strength that an adult nearby, a figure of authority, has possibly never needed to exude?

Sometimes when I contemplate having close relationships with people who are very different from me, I remember a principle I learned back in high school calculus. It had to do with approaching limits but also never reaching them. Unlike in so much of life, steeped in a mentality of goal setting and achievement, the idea was not reaching the limit as an eventuality. Nor is there ever a mathematical version of giving up by just acknowledging the limit will never be reached. This is called an asymptote: a curve that goes on infinitely approaching a line but never actually touches it. This is a role many teachers play, teaching asymptotically, trying so hard to understand our students and their lived experiences, never giving up, but also acknowledging that due to so many kinds of difference, real touching will never happen.

Of course, not all teachers are more privileged than their students, and plenty of teachers have gone through complicated and traumatic personal experiences. This is true of Benjamin, for sure. He told me in a different conversation, "I mean... how you relate to kids when you're a teacher definitely has to do with your past. My reluctance to form long term relationships with kids? Maybe it is rooted in the fact that I was in foster care till I was nine... I didn't have strong relationships." He explained that he thinks a lot about the teachers who helped him most when he was a child, "I emulate the ones who could keep a kid like me in line." In spite of his evasion of what he thinks of as closeness, he is still interested in children who are "kids like (him)," and he positions himself as a teacher who could have helped himself. How many of us, as teachers, look in our classroom particularly for that child who reminds us of our younger self? This is reasonable, fair, and practically intuitive. It just makes the question more urgent still: how much sameness does closeness require?

## Closing with Questions

There is something beautiful about a social insistence that we can be close to other people even when they are different from us. I do not think it is impossible, but I also doubt it is as easy as some cultural narratives would have it. What do you think?

These questions are oriented toward helping you bring what you thought about during this chapter into conversation with your classroom work. Consider that you do not have to have a certain answer to any of them – try to welcome and appreciate moments when you are not sure what the truth is in your reflection.

- ◆ Describe a time when you have felt really close to someone who was different from you in an important way. What did or did not allow that closeness to transcend difference?

  *It is possible that this prompt will lead you outside of your teaching practice more than it makes you think about relationships with students. Consider people you have met at various points in your life who had things in common with you but also significant differences. Think about when and how you discovered these differences, how they affected your relationship, and how you think about that person – and those differences – now.*

- Describe a time that disagreeing with someone got in the way of the strength of your relationship. Why do you think this happened?

    *This is an opposite question, one that helps you acknowledge that sometimes difference can be an obstacle to a relationship. When has this happened to you? Why do you think difference gets in the way in some kinds of relationships more than others? Does difference ever lead you to do the kind of "pretending" that Benjamin describes, or do you not find that necessary?*

- What do you think it is like for your students to disagree with you? How do you experience it when students are vocal about their disagreement?

    *Some teachers respond to disagreement more angrily than others, and some brush it off as unimportant. Try to put yourself into the mindset of a child in your class who finds themselves in disagreement with you. Would you be willing to express it? Why or why not? What might happen if you did, and what are some of the ways that could feel?*

- Do you think teachers try harder or less hard to form strong relationships with students who are different from them in key sociological ways? Why, and how does this impact teaching and learning?

    *Think about your reaction, for instance, to Finley's story. Is this story something that feels "different" from your life experiences? If so, does it make you want to pull in closer to Finley, or does it make you feel more alienated from her? In general, how do you think you respond to children whose lives, personalities, and identities are like and unlike your own, and how does this impact your overall classroom relationships?*

# 4

# Can You Be Close to Someone Who Is Just the One You're With?

My relationship with my sister Deborah is one of the closest I have ever had. Deb has at times been like a mom to me. Eleven years older, she spent plenty of time taking care of me when we were children. I remember Deb's meticulous dollhouse, the huge tissue paper flower she won at an amusement park, her adolescent obsession with clairvoyance. She was also a teacher, running summer camps for small groups of my friends, helping me encounter my first upside-down roller coaster without total panic. As we grew older, of course, our relationship evolved. For a long time, we were only in intermittent touch, our life situations just different because of age and development, with other people floating in and out. And then some time in my early adulthood, Deb and I became real friends.

We became such close friends, in fact, that when I moved back to the United States after two years in the Peace Corps, living near Deb felt intuitive. By then, she was partnered with a man I have also come to love and feel close to. I got a job near where they lived, and I had dinner with them every Friday night.

I remember driving to their house one Friday, suburban Virginia to suburban Maryland, and ending up in terrible Beltway traffic. I had to pee, and I didn't think I could make it. I called Deb from my flip phone crying and she stayed on the phone with me for 45 minutes while I inched, desperate, to their house.

That year of early adulthood was a hard one for me, and my conversations and visits with Deb and Eryq were utterly sustaining. But importantly, so was seeing them, being in a room together, sharing meals at their favorite neighborhood restaurants. Deb and Eryq started keeping sugar cereal in the house because they knew I liked to snack on it. I learned what to ask them about their days and how to rearrange their futon properly when I folded it back up.

The year of proximity changed our relationship, generating a kind of closeness we have been able to draw on like it's in the bank during the years since, as we've made our lives in different states. For the last decade or so, Deb and I have kept a standing Friday phone date, talking about everything from our aging father to our incredibly different sets of hobbies, from politics to emotional challenges we share. At the beginning of COVID, though, these phone calls fell apart. My children were out of school for an unknown duration, and time to do anything – my job, housework, errands, exercise – just felt impossible to come by. Weekly phone calls seemed an unimaginable luxury. Not only were Deb and I not really talking, but we also knew that the prospect of seeing one another was far-fetched because of the dangers of this germ we barely understood. I felt so far away from her – even though I may not have seen her during that time anyway, the fact that we absolutely couldn't made the distance feel more real. I missed her and wondered how close we could be without regular contact.

I have had relationships in my life that have been completely destroyed by that kind of temporary distancing. With Deb, things didn't go that way. Once my children went back to more structured online learning and, at long last, in-person school, we started building phone calls back into our weekly routines. Eventually, Deb came to visit for several days, and now we speak regularly again; we even see each other a few times a year. I feel so close to her. Was it the fact of our intense closeness to begin with, our many decades together, that let our relationship withstand a separation? Was it more about the concerted effort from both of us?

Separation is something so many children are dealing with all the time, every day when they go to school. They are constantly encountering new and different kinds of relationships, but none of them is their first relationship. Often, children are navigating how to handle changes and new distances in older, more primary relationships even as teachers look to them for a connection that will facilitate compliant behavior and measurable learning.

For some reason, it is common in educational discourse to frame separation as only relevant in early childhood – picture preschoolers crying at their morning goodbyes. Actually, though, all of us are dealing with separation all the time, and it impacts so many of our relationships. Separating from people I am close to is hard for me, and so is reuniting after a separation. I get anxious, even scared. What changes when we are apart from someone we love? What helps us come back together again? What if they don't love us as much, or we feel new things toward them? How does separation impact closeness?

My daughter got her first cell phone in seventh grade. Soon after she got it, our capacity to be apart from each other – really apart – diminished substantially. She texts me most days, and I text her sometimes, too. Yes, her middle school had a phone policy, her high school has an even stricter one, and the kids systematically get around it. It helps her to be in touch with me. Middle and high school are filled with bad days, awkward encounters, and challenging experiences, and it helps us both to know that when something is awry, she can usually find me.

But of course, I am also aware of the critique of this kind of parent/child relationship. No one my age had any such tools at our disposal. And there is this general normative view that kids should be able to function for a day, and later much longer, without a direct pipeline to their parents. Does it actually make her more anxious, more dependent to know that I am on tap? The capacities of now-mundane technologies like smartphones raise so many questions about closeness and the nature of relationships. They facilitate closeness and also make closeness more frantic. They let us connect with people constantly, all over the place, but they also make us lonelier, less likely to engage with what is right there. Some elementary students are already managing this aspect of relationships, and just about all of them know that it is out there, that adults, including their teachers, have that device right on hand.

My daughter, my sister Deb – these are just two of the important figures in my life with whom I am constantly navigating a tenuous relationship between closeness and proximity. How close can we be to a person when they are somewhere else? If we turn to the person who is right there, what does that do to the people we love, but who are far away? What it means to love the one you're just accidentally close to gets at a set of questions a lot of children are encountering, usually unaddressed, during their time in school.

An interesting thing about the demand that teachers form strong relationships with children is that it ignores the ways this might impact, or even simply *seem* to impact, other relationships in the child's life. When the teacher works to establish closeness, she is not necessarily thinking about who else in the child's world she is mirroring, invoking, contradicting, or displacing. Few children are consciously aware of this kind of dynamic, but most children are, on some level, thinking about the different relationships in their lives and how they interact with the relationships they encounter in schools. In this chapter, I look at what children may be thinking about closeness as related to who is and isn't right there, and how they are contemplating and working through the question of what it means to be close to someone who is far away.

## Laila Is Far Away from Home

In the last chapter, I described how Ainsley thinks of herself as teaching close to home. Laila, by contrast, describes herself as teaching far away from "home," and this is part of what can make teaching exciting for her. When we spoke about her family, she did say that she feels close to them – but that she also finds them challenging to be around. "I honestly find it so much easier" to teach without them nearby, she explained. "My family and I have a very difficult relationship, so being a bit further away from them is beneficial for me."

For Laila, physical distance begets emotional distance, and it is an emotional distance she likes. Being further away from people with whom she might be assumed to have a close relationship, but who she also finds problematic, helps her become more of her own person. Many children experience school as this kind of opportunity, too. The physical distance helps Laila figure herself out and form closer relationships to the people she does find nearby, "I find my own chosen family," she said.

I asked her where she finds this chosen family. She described friends from college who she "love(s) like family." She also explained, "and I find my chosen family within my own classroom." The closeness in her classroom is something that helps Laila, in other words, and so she is motivated to form relationships with students not just for their benefit but also for her own. This strikes me as so complicated. On the one hand, it seems like a teacher using students almost inappropriately. Shouldn't a teacher be somehow beyond needing that kind of gratification from their students? On the other hand, isn't this a fairly universal phenomenon – that we can't be present with others in such a constant way without needing something from them?

Laila also talked about what it felt like to teach when she lived closer to her family of origin. "I used to teach after school when I lived at home… I found it so much more draining and stressful returning home to a house with my family." This speaks to the emotional drain of relationships that can be unhelpful or even harmful, especially when in close proximity. Laila gives a lot of herself every day in school, and it makes sense that she wants the rest of her hours to be filled with relationships that do not "drain" her. Plenty of children also have this experience. They are expending energy all day, much of it relational energy, and then they also have to go home and manage in challenging, sometimes draining situations. What they experience in one venue is undoubtedly going to influence what they bring to the other.

For Laila, teaching far away from the place she still thinks of as "home" is helpful, but she also recognizes that this is a distance she has intentionally cultivated and benefited from. She finds it difficult to contemplate simultaneously maintaining close "chosen family" relationships with students, friends, and colleagues, and managing her family of origin and their version of closeness: what they want from her and who they want her to be. I can very much relate to what Laila is describing, because I too have established a lot of distance, geographical combined with emotional, from parts of my family I find draining and painful. I know how freeing it can be to separate in this way, even as I carry resulting sadness, guilt, and regret. I also know how complicated and potentially fraught it is to then turn to others, perhaps particularly children, and ask them for closeness. Each member of a classroom is navigating their own set of situations like these, a whole network of relationships near and far, helpful and harmful and everything in between. Are they missing the family they left at home? Are they so grateful to have left them behind? When we meet up in a classroom, what are we looking for from one another, and what, or whom, are we replacing?

## Rabbit's Mom Didn't Come

Almost all of the children in Ainsley's class spoke about their families when I interviewed them about close relationships in their lives. Recall that many of these children have experienced substantial separations from their families of origin, have been or are currently in foster care, and have consequently had to do a lot of thinking – albeit partly unconscious – about what it means to trust someone to take care of you. Teachers often have very little information about the stories behind these circumstances, and Ainsley is no exception.

Rabbit, a white boy in Ainsley's morning group, has been in foster care twice, for reasons Ainsley is not sure about, with two different families. For his whole year in Ainsley's class, though, he lived with his birth parents and a baby brother. Rabbit started our interview by telling me about his two best friends and how much he likes playing hockey with them. I thought he was going to explain that this is why he feels close to his friends, but he actually used a story about hockey to explain why he feels close to his parents. "One time?" he said,

> We were playing hockey and the puck hit me hard. I bounced on the ground two times on my back. I was about to cry but I didn't want to. But my mom, she saw, and then she got me an ice pack.

"That must have felt pretty good," I responded.

"Yeah," Rabbit went on, "Well, first I didn't want the ice pack because it didn't really hurt. But then, I put it on, and then I was crying. I was about to cry, then I was crying and my mom was there."

There is so much vulnerability in being close to someone, and at the same time, vulnerability in front of a person is often part of what brings us closer, lets us relax our defenses and helps us remember that no matter how independent and strong we feel, we still need others. Rabbit was describing this emotional cycle through his story: grateful to his mom, comfortable enough to cry, ambivalent about that level of emotional disclosure.

I asked Rabbit if there is anyone at school who he feels close to. He answered right away, "Ms. Spencer [the principal], the one that sits down at the big desk. In front of the office in front of the school."

When I wondered what it is about Ms. Spencer that made Rabbit feel close to her, he launched into another story. "Well, one time, when I was in kindergarten, my mom was deep asleep. And Ms. Spencer was nice to me." I waited, and he continued, "She was SO deep asleep – my mom – that she didn't wake up, she didn't come for me."

This story sounded scary, and I told him so. "No, it was NOT scary," Rabbit emphasized, "that was NOT scary for me."

I asked what Ms. Spencer did when Rabbit's mom did not come, and his answer was fast and simple. "She gave me snacks, she was nice to me, she waited with me and then she gave me some more snacks." Then he shrugged. "If you be nice to people, then they be nice to you," he added with a nod.

Rabbit had to rely on someone at school to "be nice" to him when his mom was unavailable. Ms. Spencer knew just the right way to help, and even though this happened over a year ago, her kindness stuck with Rabbit. But I wondered what it does to his relationships with teachers and other adults in school to feel like they are standing in for his mom, who he feels so close to and who he knows he will need to rely on for some time to come, even though he has also experienced disappointments from her. "Is it nice," I asked Rabbit, "When you feel close to someone at school?"

Rabbit shrugged, "It's okay, yeah," he asked, "but you have to be good if you want the ones at school to be nice to you."

Rabbit has had to rely a lot on kindness, food, and different sorts of intervention from his teachers and other adults at school. This does not make him unusual in a society that offers children and families little support and plenty of ongoing pressure. Still, it is important to him to frame that kind of love as conditional, contrasted to the closeness he feels for his parents, even when they aren't or can't be right there. Maybe Rabbit feels he can be most vulnerable and complicated around his mom, or maybe he feels protective of her, intuitively understanding the kinds of judgment she must face, including from adults at school and potentially, in his view, from me.

Most teachers understand that they both do and don't operate in the place of parents or other caregivers while children are at school. But I'm not sure we spend enough time thinking about how present those closest people are for children during much of the day, how even though they aren't literally in the room with us, the fact of their closeness, their significance in a child's world, has a lot to do with how the child relates to us and perceives our efforts to relate to them. If they accept our snacks, are they betraying their mom? If they listen to our instructions and ideas, do they have to make choices about the instructions and ideas of other close, but not proximate, figures? This is another reminder that when we ask children for relationships, we are not asking for any small thing. We owe it to them to remember the large cast of characters who might be influencing the nature of any connection that emerges.

## Cuddling on the Couch

Simone, a white girl also from Ainsley's class, spoke to me about her intense feelings of closeness with her family. I asked Simone to draw me a picture of a time she felt close to someone else at school (Figure 4.1).

**FIGURE 4.1** Simone feels like she is closest to someone when she's cuddling with her mom on the couch and Mickey is somewhere nearby.

Simone asked about her twin brother. "Can I draw a picture with Mickey, even though he's not in my class?" I told her she could draw whatever came to mind, and she told me she was going to draw a picture of herself cuddling with Mickey.

As she drew, she narrated, "We're usually downstairs when we're cuddling," Simone told me, "and Mama is there with us too. This is on the couch." Simone thought for a moment, then continued drawing and talking. "Actually," she said, "I think Mickey isn't there in this picture. It's just me and Mama."

In this way, Simone cleverly morphed an assignment to draw herself with someone she feels close to at school, to drawing herself cuddling with her mom on the couch. "Me and Mickey," she continued, "see, WE'RE usually downstairs when we have our ARGUES."

"Is that why Mickey isn't in the picture?" I asked.

"No," Simone responded, "I just wanted to draw me and Mama cuddling. It feels so good." After a moment, she decided to add Mickey into the picture after all. "He's actually here," she explained, putting him off to the side. "But he's giving me a hairy eyeball. Because he didn't want to cuddle." Simone exhibited such a masterful set of moves in her drawing and telling, using her twin brother as a middleman between school and home. For her, closeness is going to be about family.

Then she takes it a step further, actually pushing her brother right out of the scene and focusing on her connection with her mom. And she explains what closeness is: it's cuddling, literal physical touch. "It feels so good" to her. Maybe it is guilt that pushes her to put Mickey back in, or maybe it is a true sense of missing him in the picture. Either way, for Simone, closeness isn't about what goes on at school, and she seems perfectly at peace with that.

There are plenty of people, like Laila, who appreciate the opportunities work and school afford to form close relationships that make up for some sort of deficit or imbalance in the other relationships in their world. There are people like Ainsley, who want these relationships because they make teaching and learning more exciting, or just because they make school feel warmer and more fun than it otherwise might. And there are also plenty of people, like Simone, who are more or less fine in school but want and need very little from their teachers emotionally, because for them, the relationships that count are the ones who are, during the school day, far away.

Interestingly, Ainsley described Simone as one of her most difficult students to connect with. "I struggle gaining a relationship with her," Ainsley reported,

> I feel no matter how much I try to be her friend, gain her trust, or help her through a challenging situation, she builds a wall against me. She doesn't laugh at my silliness, doesn't want to talk to me on a more intimate level, doesn't want or accept my help in academics.

Ainsley grew increasingly upset describing this impasse. I asked her how the situation impacts her, and she reflected,

> The rejection at first made me want to try harder but at some point it made me want to try less or not at all. The rejection from her made me no longer want to be her friend but simply go about the role of being her teacher.

Remember from Chapter 2 that the role or "mode" of teacher is meaningful to Ainsley, and what it means is something in opposition to closeness. I offered my understanding of that defensive move and asked Ainsley how it has gone with Simone recently. She sighed. "Rejection hurts no matter how old you are, even if that rejection is from a six-year-old," she confided.

I could not agree with Ainsley more. In fact, I find age totally irrelevant to how rejection can feel. "I haven't quite figured out why this is," she went on.

> I have these theories I have developed that some children have had adults in their life they can't trust and it makes them isolate themselves from other adults. Or... the adults in a child's life are simply an adult, a breadwinner, a superior, not a friend, and then children have a difficult time accepting that some adults are trying to be their friend and equal.

Ainsley is right again. It is true for children, just as it is true for all of us, that our relationships with one person are impacted heavily by our relationships with other people. Laila spoke about the same phenomenon when she described how she connects with her students. These relationships, Laila described, "...very much echo my other relationships!... I echo what other teachers have done for me, or what I want... and it's also a lot like how I value my friendships, and I hold those friendships very close, too." Many of us who struggle within one relationship – for example, to trust, to be vulnerable, to ask for what we need – can trace that struggle to our earliest relationships and how they continue to impact our personalities and fears. Ainsley wasn't the first to develop this theory, but because it is one that illustrates itself in such personal, intimate ways, maybe it is something each of us needs to figure out in our own context again and again.

At the same time, adults tend to see pathology any time a child is reluctant to connect when, sometimes, the child actually just doesn't want a relationship with the teacher. It is too hard to tell the details of Simone's relationships with other adults in her world from the small details she offered me, but it does not sound like these are distant, untrusting, or problematic relationships. Instead, it sounds like Simone, who gets by in school with very few obvious struggles, really misses her mom. She wants to be home on that couch, cuddling, with Mickey near but not too near. She is pining, and also she knows just how good that physical closeness with someone who adores her can be. It translates into a challenge for Ainsley, but for Simone, maybe it is okay. She has figured out that her closest people don't have to be the ones who are right there. They can be people she shares history with, like I do with Deb, people she can recreate in her mind on a moment's notice.

## Xavier Misses His Moms

First graders missing their parents may seem less surprising to some readers than fifth graders feeling the same way, until we stop and think about how much all of us, at different points throughout our difficult days in the world, wish to be closer to the people who make us feel the safest. This anecdote from Laila and Benjamin's class describes Xavier, a child known by everyone at the school for his frequent, sometimes aggressive, emotional outbursts. Xavier, a white boy, carries a dossier of diagnoses and works with several support staff. His moms adopted him as an infant, and he is an only child.

*Toward the end of a math group rotation, Xavier, who has been working with Benjamin in the corner, begins to make noticeable noise. I am sitting closer to where Laila has Rosie, Edo, and Sam together playing a math game, but I notice that when Xavier starts to rumble, the tone in the room shifts slightly. Many of the kids have been chatting and grow quieter. Laila keeps working with her group but seems to be carefully watching Benjamin's side of the room.*

*Xavier rises and tosses a marker across the room. He stomps his foot. Benjamin, keeping calm, gets up and puts one hand on the small of Xavier's back. "Do you want to take a little walk?" Benjamin asks. Laila also stands, gesturing for her students to keep playing the game. She comes over to Xavier, and she and Benjamin exchange a look that appears to mean, "Let's trade." Benjamin takes Laila's place at the math game.*

*Laila puts her hand on Xavier's back now, and his body looks dysregulated. He is stomping, crying, and flailing. "I miss my MOMS!" he shouts.*

*"Was math getting kind of hard?" Laila asks as she guides him toward the hallway.*

*For a moment, Xavier keeps writhing, but he relaxes slightly and starts to walk with her. "I want to go HOME!" he exclaims. Laila keeps moving her arm in circles on his back.*

*"I bet you do really miss them," she says. They reach the door and Xavier slumps down on the floor of the hallway, leaning forward so his whole face is obscured. Laila sits down beside him and waits. "I want to go home, I want to go home, I want to go home," Xavier keeps repeating. After about five minutes, he stops. Laila sends him for a drink of water, and soon he returns to class.*

In general, Laila's relationship with Xavier functions like this: she has an intuitive sense of how much touch and intervention he needs, having watched him closely and worked with other students prone to big meltdowns. She and Benjamin have also established a system in their class where the rest of the children know to keep going and let Xavier work things through. What could have been a major disruption is instead a private, gentle de-escalation. Xavier barely engages with Laila in this episode, but he does respond to her and let her help him move to a physical place where he can calm himself.

The wanting to go home, though, is wrenching, surprising, and at the same time, completely understandable. There are so many different ways to look at this scene. One way is: Xavier is a little immature and dysregulated. His behavior seems more like what many adults would expect from a toddler or kindergartner. This is symptomatic of his various diagnoses, and one of the school's supposed jobs is to help him learn more self-control and become increasingly independent at regulating down when things get stressful. Laila's patient, loving care shows that the two of them have a strong relationship, and Xavier trusts her enough to let her get him back to a place of equilibrium. School can be genuinely difficult, but children need to learn to weather challenges like a hard math activity without resorting to tantrums.

This perspective is valid. So is a different narrative about the whole scene: Xavier has a really close connection with his moms. Home is the place in the world where he feels safest and most comfortable. He spends a lot of his school day wishing he were actually there. So, in fact, do a lot, though not all, of his classmates. So do a lot of adults when they are at work! How wonderful that in the midst of multiple cultural narratives about difficult home lives, there are also children who love to be home, love the connections they have there so much that what exists in school is actually incredibly difficult by comparison.

Children sometimes have to figure out what it means to be far away from people they love. This is a kind of understanding notably absent from learning rubrics or SEL frameworks. It is not a quick one-off on a checklist but rather, for many of us, a lifelong set of lessons, hiccups, and borderline successes. What happens when you can't be with the one you love? Maybe instead of just being unregulated and overwhelmed, Xavier is also fortunate to have relatively unfettered access to his feelings about home and connection. It is kind and compassionate of Laila, whose own experience of home and family is generally much more negative, to honor them so patiently.

Neither of these perspectives is the only feasible one, but the point I make by sharing them is this: how teachers and the educational community perceive a child's behavior might not always impact the teacher's specific response in one moment. Laila might have "handled" Xavier's outburst the same way whether her goal was to get him under control for the sake of compliance and an overall calm and functioning classroom, or whether her goal was to help him through this moment of acute longing. It was a loving, empathetic, and generally admirable response.

But I also think the ways we interpret these stories inside our own minds actually matter. They matter because teachers are usually looking for something from children relationally. When we try to approach honesty with ourselves about what we are seeking, we can be more generous overall about the infinite relational foibles and mishaps that inevitably arise. Any teacher can choose to turn a fifth grader missing their parents into a pathology that needs some sort of intervention, but what are we offering ourselves, in that case, about whatever challenges in closeness and separation we experience?

It is easy to forget that when we offer a child our relationship, we are not just giving them something – we are also asking a lot of them. There are children who will accept our relationships with gratitude, but there are also children – plenty of them – who have to do unconscious internal weighing about what that acceptance might mean in concert with every other relationship in their world. Xavier is figuring this out: can he be close to Benjamin, to Laila, to the rest of the children – and still be allowed to miss his moms? I think he can, but it makes teaching him more complicated. It is hard at any one moment to be sure how much of him is there, how much somewhere else longing to be with the people who love him most. Is that true for all of us?

Relationships with people who are not right there are challenging, and how they interact with the relationships right in front of us – the ones we're with – is something that affects most of our behavior and reactions every day. It is also worth remembering that only a small minority of relationships between teachers and students last longer than the confines of one or two school years. Children usually know this, and they have to factor in the inevitability of those goodbyes as they invest, or choose not to invest, in the relationship.

What kind of education happens for the rest of the class when Laila and Benjamin both move their focus to Xavier? As happens in all classrooms sometimes, Xavier's behavior takes over the curriculum. The small group switches teachers, and everyone gets a chance to watch what will happen with a child who is flailing and screaming, a child who badly wants to go home. When I was in Laila and Benjamin's class for these kinds of episodes, I often thought about the massive advantages to co-teachers and children with two teachers. Not only can they keep continuity for the rest of the class and still give Xavier a lot of attention, but also, they can spot each other: if one situation is really not going to work for Benjamin, who has less patience than Laila for homesickness, he can pass it to her.

Over the course of the year, I saw Laila and Benjamin help each other that way a lot of times, I think often without even being completely aware they were doing it. They learned, like many good partnerships across domains in life, who was better suited for which tasks. Most teachers do not have that kind of relationship available, and that can become another kind of longing or missing in a classroom, one with a less specific object. Sometimes I wondered if the seemingly heteronormative parenting dynamic between Laila and Benjamin, each taking on these stereotypical gender roles in relation to children, was challenging for Xavier, coming from a queer family. Did that make him miss home more?

Children are always watching and considering how teachers relate to their peers. Over time, what they do with these observations impacts not only individual children's behavior, but also the sense of community in a classroom. I have been in plenty of classrooms where children have strong relationships with one another specifically because they feel like they need to have each other's backs in relation to a very stern, punitive teacher. Ironically, this can lead to a wonderful sense of peer community, though certainly with significant tradeoffs. It reminds me of how my sisters and I would cluster together most tightly when our parents most viciously fought, or when we perceived them as being particularly mean.

I have also been in classrooms where children have picked up on a teacher's irritation with one or a few students and feel so connected to the teacher that they privately also target and shame the "troublemakers." "Sammy's bad," a child will tell me, "he's always getting in trouble." This same child might actually adore Sammy, but they have done a calculation that ostracizing him will help them stay in the teacher's good graces. There is a lot of constantly moving internal understanding of relationships within a group that comes from group members watching and considering individual and smaller subgroup interactions. Since every member of the group is also bringing in so many other relationships as well – the moms, the siblings, the grandparents, and so on, who are there without being right there – the total web of relationships and learning in a classroom grows quite unfathomable. The idea of controlling it – of "forming relationships" as an item on a management checklist – starts to seem a bit laughable. Maybe different children have to decide in their own ways whether they want to connect just because you're the one they're with.

## Closing with Questions

Thinking back on the ideas we have discussed in this chapter, consider the ways proximity, distance, longing, missing, and separation might be affecting your own relationships, as well as the ways children in your class relate to you. These questions are designed to help you apply these understandings to your teaching, hopefully in a way that lets you find generosity and compassion toward children and yourself.

- What are some ways students in your classroom are experiencing their relationships with their families and other important people in their lives over the course of the school day? How does this affect your relationships with these children?

  *As we saw with Xavier, Simone, and other children in this chapter, every child brings a slightly different picture of their family into the classroom. Every teacher also has a different sense of who their students' families are – some of us may know next to nothing about our children's family lives, and some of us might know a lot. How do you find out about your students' lives outside of schools? How can you stop yourself from making assumptions about a child's family? How much do you think your students' relationships outside the classroom impact what they bring to the classroom every day?*

- What is it like for you to teach when you might be far away from the people you feel closest to?

> *Just as students bring different relationships with their families into the classroom, teachers do the same. What are some times in your practice when you have really wished to be somewhere else, with someone else, or at least closer to people who aren't right there? How do you think this kind of missing or distance impacts the relationships you have with your students?*

- What are some times you have looked for closeness from your students, but had trouble achieving it? How has this affected your classroom practice?

  > *Ainsley describes the frustration of wanting a relationship with Simone that Simone feels unavailable for or uninterested in. When have you had a difficult time connecting with a child? What do you attribute it to, and how did you respond? What do you see as some of teachers' responsibilities when we find ourselves wanting specific things from our students?*

- How does your work with specific individual kids look to the rest of the classroom, in your opinion? How might working with one child impact, in both positive and negative ways, your overall sense of classroom community?

  > *Think about how the other children in Benjamin and Laila's class internalize Xavier's outbursts. What are some times in your teaching that you have wondered about how an individual child, and your work with them, is impacting the rest of the class? How do your thoughts around this topic impact your actual work with individual children?*

# 5

# Can You Be Close to Someone and Want Them to Change?

Have you ever seen the musical *Guys and Dolls?* Among other things, it features a hilarious song where two female main characters, Sarah and Adelaide, are discussing the men they hope to marry, each of them wishing he would change in significant ways. One cautions the other that you might as well get married first and only *then* focus on how you want to change your brand new spouse.

Obviously this is tongue-in-cheek, but I would venture a guess that most married and partnered people can identify with the sentiments it reflects. Sometimes, you can really love someone but still wish they were a little different – a little closer to the picture of the ideal version of themselves that you have in your mind.

Seeing a person for who they are and accepting them that way? Lately I think that is what love means, but also that it is aspirational, time-consuming, and far from simple for most of us. It is also not static. We might feel like someone we love is just right today, or in a particular situation. The next day, they might embarrass us in public or we might become incredibly frustrated with some specific trait: indecision, fashion choices, bossiness, and so forth. What does the wish for another person to change do to our sense of closeness to that person? Conversely, what does the knowledge that someone wants you to change do to your closeness to them?

These questions are generally difficult, but I think they can be particularly challenging in teaching. I have found that in other kinds of relationships, gradually releasing the desire to change another person helps quite a bit. I have more harmony with people who I accept for who they are, and I think it is the rare person who happily changes in response to someone else's wishes. As for others' wish that I change? It depends! Sometimes I really try, and other times I reach into my store of confidence and deepest sense of self and decide, it's just not going to happen, that isn't who I am.

In school, though, a teacher's desire for students to change is built into the job description. What's more, as SEL curricula and other offshoots of character education take firmer hold, the changes teachers are likely to wish for in students go beyond wanting our students to become stronger readers, writers, and mathematicians. We are tasked with helping them develop as whole people, which may sound lovely but also embeds an assumption that something about them as they are isn't going to cut it. Part of teaching means wanting the student to become meaningfully different, but this can be paradoxical when it comes to developing close relationships. This chapter invites teachers to think about what it means to be in a relationship with someone who wants them to change, too.

Many elementary school teachers are drawn to work with children because of the sense of openness and acceptance children bring. This stands out to me when, once a year, I teach a class that brings together students pursuing elementary and early childhood licenses with those focused on secondary schools. So often, the middle and high school teachers are taken aback by the physical load their elementary colleagues take on (wiping noses and tightening straps on snow pants), by the whining and concreteness of younger children, by the more frequent contact with parents. Teachers of younger children, by contrast, generally sum up their position succinctly: at least they don't have to be with teenagers.

When I have pushed on this sentiment, it usually comes down to a tremendous concern about the judgmental attitude so many adolescents, albeit often defensively, exude. A person who wants to work with elementary students is often – though of course this is a generalization – a person who longs to be loved, looked up to overtly, and accepted for who they are. Let me be clear: this is not a bad thing! Sometimes, it just means being more in touch with a very basic human longing. Teachers of young children do often get this gratification from their students, and that can facilitate the relationship, but it also adds a layer of complexity to how much change these teachers, in turn, try to elicit – often more than their secondary colleagues, who see students for shorter periods of time and tend to be less involved in character work.

This chapter explores the question of what happens with closeness when one person wants another to change. We will see how Ainsley, Laila, and Benjamin think about this theme, as well as how they work for change in their students and how their students respond. One idea that recurred as I explored this question was around how many goals teachers set for their students without being certain about how children themselves want to learn, grow, evolve – or stay the same. What would it mean to teach without being sure of a child's desired outcome, of their own capacity or, more importantly, wish for change?

## Ainsley Contemplates Judgement

Again and again, Ainsley told me how important it is for her that her students feel loved and cared for in her classroom. Love, as a concept, permeates her practice, and she explicitly tells her students that she loves them multiple times each day. Many of her students brought this up unsolicited in interviews, telling me that one thing they like about their teacher is how much she loves them. I was often flabbergasted at how loved and safe many of Ainsley's students felt under her care, particularly because so many of them have experienced trauma related to attachment and separation. Even though love is impossibly hard to define, even though there were definitely children her strategies helped more than others, Ainsley is accomplishing a massive feat by bringing the language and physical sense of love into so many children's worlds.

When I talked to Ainsley about how her teaching relationships are and are not like other relationships in her world, she started describing general social and interpersonal insecurity. "I am the type of person," she said, "that has always, always struggled with trusting that I am loved in many of my personal relationships." I asked her what she meant, and she went on,

> Well, I am constantly wondering if I am making my parents proud... or I will often assume my friends are talking about me behind my back... or even with strangers, when I walk past someone in the store or whatever, I think, what do they think about my outfit? What have they heard about me? What are they saying when I walk away?

How many of us have worries similar to Ainsley's? As she described these, I thought of how hard I have had to work, over so many years, and in and out of therapy, to even skate on the edge of not plunging into these kinds of insecurities – and that's without having grown up on social media. Do these worries make Ainsley a particular "type of person," with concerning problems? Or do they just make her a person?

I expected that Ainsley would transition from describing these struggles to saying that she also worries a lot about what her students think of her. I sometimes struggled that way with elementary children and I was teaching, and I certainly do with my college students today. It is usually a kind of nonspecific, "Do they like me? Am I doing this right?" Ainsley went in a different direction, though. "There is something about working with children that those same feelings don't apply to my relationship with them," she explained,

> It is not that I don't overthink whether or not they like me, because sometimes I do. But I understand that they don't hold me to a standard. So it's easier for me to talk to them, easier to be myself. Children don't understand or use judgment in the same ways we have learned to judge as an adult... so there isn't pressure to be anything other than yourself around them because they are simply themselves all the time, unapologetically.

Ainsley's explanation makes so much sense. I have often thought similar things about children, and so have many early childhood and elementary teachers I have spoken with around this theme. I remember when my daughter was younger and I led her Girl Scout troop. I had no problem at all acting goofy, getting sloppy in my arts and crafts, learning outdoor skills as I went along, and planning all sorts of different activities for a group of ten second-grade girls. Once in a while, though, we would do excursions or special workshops that parents wanted to come along for. With the parents – my peers, and in some cases even my friends – there, I felt so self-conscious, so aware that they might wish for me to do things differently or be a different way. It was oppressive. It actually made me worse at the job.

There are many logical flaws about this formulation, though. Plenty of children do judge, do fervently wish their teachers were different. Children wish their teachers were more fun, offered extra recess more frequently, moved faster or slower through new material – and yes, wore different colors, funnier jewelry, and more or less perfume. So what is it about the fact of *children* wanting those changes that makes the judgement feel different? Is this again a question of power, as we discussed in Chapter 2? Because children have so little power over teachers, ultimately, maybe we worry less about their wishes for us. Or maybe it is some sense of forgiveness and pleasant forgetfulness we get. This, I think, is what Ainsley gestures toward when she says, "they are simply themselves all the time, unapologetically."

And here is the thorny part of the question this chapter poses: that may not actually be true. Teachers ask children to change all the time in schools, and I'm not sure how many of them really feel unapologetically themselves. I have spoken to many children over the years who are questioning just like their adult counterparts: I am doing it wrong, people don't like me, I don't belong here, I can't quite keep up.

Why is it so important for so many adults to maintain this partial fiction that children have easier access to their unapologetic selves? It is really hard to figure out how much anyone in a classroom relationship wants or pushes for change in themselves or anyone else. For Ainsley, it is the *illusion* of her students' absence of judgement that lets her feel closer to them. She can feel a deeper, more vulnerable and open connection to someone when she thinks they accept her as she is, when she feels they don't want her to change. Ironically, she does ask her students to change and grow as part of the teaching contract.

## I'm Happy with My Friends

In Chapter 1, we talked about how much the social worlds of childhood take priority in many children's minds when it comes to close relationships. Several of the children I spoke with specifically referenced ways they can be themselves with friends, because friends do not expect them to grow up, try harder, or change. This, for some children, was conducive to a special closeness.

Jack, from Ainsley's class, reminded me several times that he loves his teacher and he knows she loves him. Like so many

**FIGURE 5.1** Jack felt especially close to BJ when they happily built a tower together.

other children, though, he also included his understanding that she wants him to "be good." "So that's why I try to never be bad," he explained, "she likes me better when I'm good."

When I asked Jack to draw a picture of feeling close to another person at school, he drew himself sitting with his friend BJ (Figure 5.1).

"That's me on that side," he said, pointing at the figure on the left, "And that's BJ. And we builded that tower." He gestured at the tall tower between them. I asked Jack why he and BJ feel so close when they build together. "I'm smiling at him and he's smiling back at me because we're happy," he explained. "We're happy when we're having fun together because I like him to be having fun and he likes me to be having fun. I'm happy with my friends."

Thinking about what Jack had just told me about Ainsley, I asked him whether he thinks BJ wants him to be good. Jack laughed and shook his head. "It's like…," he thought for a moment, "it's like, we're good together when we're at school and when we're outside we're good, we're bad, we're having fun together, we're just DOING it."

I understood Jack to mean that with BJ, he doesn't have to think about how he is being or who he is being. He is simply *being*, and that is something that makes him feel especially close to BJ. Of course, not every interaction between two people can be like that. If teachers just let students do and be whatever they wanted all the time, it would fundamentally alter the project and nature of school.

What's more, in a group of people as big as a classroom community, the way one person wants to be is incredibly likely to disrupt the way another person does. Often, I see this play out along sociological power dynamics, so a white child "just being" is disruptive to a child of color, a boy to a girl. There have been major societal conversations about this theme in the last decade in the United States. If one person's "just being" is not wearing a mask, but that can lead to another person's contracting a potentially fatal disease, the question can be framed alternately as one of integral social responsibility or one of personal freedom. I am inclined to come down on the social responsibility side, and extending this analogy to other parts of life reminds me that being allowed to just be myself with no expectation of change carries a lot of meaning for how I and the people around me inhabit the world. This is, to my mind, an unreasonable centering of the individual, typical of US cultural ideals, and there are innumerable examples of just how wrong it can go. It is no utopian vision, and because of that, it is not necessarily a problem that Ainsley triggers the "be good" response in Jack.

At the same time, there is something important about acknowledging the way teachers by definition want children to change. I love you, but I want you to: read better, sit more quietly, try harder, open up more, do math faster, eat healthier, and so on. Of course this does something to closeness! How could it not? Again, it leaves me wondering if the language of relationship does not quite fit what goes on between child and teacher all the time. A teacher might feel close to a child, but their vision of that child is different from who the child is and maybe even who the child wants to be. How much the teacher gets to decide on the vision of who the child should be is a substantial question, and as with so many philosophical questions in teaching, I think it is less important to answer it than to do a better job acknowledging simply that the question exists.

## Who Reorganized This Bin?

*Daniel, a white boy, and Grace, a Latina girl, are partners for a science project about endangered species of the Northeast. Grace has been out of the room for the first part of science, because she plays clarinet in the school band and they had a last-minute rehearsal. She comes back to the classroom to find Daniel sitting with Laila, working on their poster together.*

"I'm back," Grace tells them.

*Laila smiles,* "How was band?"

*Grace shrugs,* "It was okay." *Laila gets up and gestures for Grace to sit with Daniel.* "Hey, Daniel," *Grace says. He nods at her.*

*Daniel pushes a pile of index cards over to Grace without saying anything and then focuses back on the poster he is decorating, drawing tiny, cartoon chipmunk faces around the border. Laila moves to check in with another group, and Grace shuffles through the cards Daniel has given her. Then she tells Daniel,* "I'm going to go get my supply bin."

*Daniel answers,* "Okay, yeah. We can get the owl pictures ready today."

*Grace smiles and says,* "I'm good with owls." *She goes over to the shelves where each child has a bin of supplies, including the colored pencils many children are using to draw and label diagrams of animals. When Grace finds her bin, though, she is startled.* "My pencils are on top!" *she says, first to herself and then again more loudly,* "My pencils are on top, and I know I put them on the bottom!"

*She looks at Daniel quizzically, and he rolls his eyes, then points in Laila's direction.* "Ms. Audrey!" *Grace calls out,* "Who reorganized this bin?"

*Laila laughs.* "Grace," *she says, not getting up from the other group where she is sitting,* "It was filled with trash and I threw a bunch of it away. You have to keep your things more organized, it's impossible to find anything and that's why you guys are behind on your poster. Get your pencils – at least you can see them now – and get to work."

*Grace, chastened, takes her supply bin and goes back to sit with Daniel, but I notice that for the rest of the period, she shuffles her pencils round and round without drawing anything.*

As a mom and as a teacher, I have plenty of sympathy with Laila's reorganization of Grace's things. Children can be unthinkably sloppy – and that is my impression even as someone who is not particularly tidy. At the end of the day, when they have all gone home, the teacher is often left with a chaotic scene that they feel calmer rectifying. A lot of teachers also think we are helping children when we remind them – sometimes the hard way, by throwing out things that seem like trash – the importance of keeping space organized. This can seem like a life lesson, a part of subtle character education that many teachers do really prioritize: take care of your things, or you will lose them. How often do you hear teachers complaining about how little respect children show for the material world of the classroom and school? Teachers often know better than children how much effort goes into procuring and maintaining the supplies it takes to move through a curriculum productively.

Grace learns something else here, too. She clearly had some kind of system in place, or she would not have noticed that her pencils were no longer where she left them. It might have looked like she just shoved everything in the bin, but she knew what she was doing, and it mattered to her. Her system was not satisfying to Laila. Laila wanted something different for Grace, wanted Grace to organize differently, throw her trash away, be a little different. (As a side note, I have often noticed that what adults and children perceive to be trash is actually categorically different;

the very definition of that word seems to evolve as people age.) Laila wants change, and what's more, it doesn't really register with her that this is at all a serious ask. Grace has to digest this. She will, but it will take some time, and it may have implications for her sense of a relationship to both herself and to Laila in the meantime.

## I'm Not Mad at You

An especially difficult aspect of teachers wanting change from children has to do with the fact that many children have little control over the circumstances of their lives. This vignette, also from Laila and Benjamin's class, shows an interaction where this comes up and a child has to figure out how to make the most of a situation where different adults in his life are giving him different messages.

*This math period, Laila is working with the whole group, while Benjamin pulls one student at a time to talk through work they have missed or concepts they are struggling with. After sending Honorah back to her group, he taps Colin gently on the shoulder. "Colin," Benjamin says, "come back to my table, will you?"*

*Colin glances wistfully at the game Laila is projecting on the Smartboard. Then he looks at Benjamin and says, "Okay, okay." He gets up good-naturedly and follows Benjamin to his table. "What are we going to do?" he asks.*

*Benjamin speaks quietly, so the other children in the class can't hear what they are talking about. He says to Colin, "It seems like you've been having a really hard time in math lately."*

*Colin hangs his head.*

*"I'm not mad at you, Colin," Benjamin assures him, "I just wanted to talk to you about it. Why do you think you've been having such a hard time?"*

*Colin, clearly ashamed, looks down at the floor, kicking his shoe lightly against the leg of a desk. "I dunno," he whispers.*

*"Well, I can tell you what I think," Benjamin goes on, "I think it's because you have missed SO much math lately."*

*Colin still doesn't say anything, and his kicking stills.*

*"Hey!" Benjamin says, trying to get Colin to make eye contact, which he continues to avoid. "Listen! I'm not mad at you, okay? I'm just explaining why you're struggling. Lately you've been missing a lot of school! You've been coming in super late, and then you miss math... and this is why you're struggling. Okay?"*

*Colin still says nothing. He holds completely still, continuing to gaze down at the floor. Benjamin continues, "You need to be here. This is why you're struggling, okay? You need to be here so you can hear the big lesson, and then so you can practice."*

*Having apparently said his piece, and realizing he is not going to get a clear response from Colin, Benjamin lets up. "Okay," he says, "let's take a look at these fractions." Once they dive into the work, Colin finally looks up. He works slowly but willingly until Benjamin sends him back to his desk.*

I remember vividly how frustrating it is for a teacher when a child does not come to school. Schools have attendance records to maintain, and funding, accreditation, and overall reputation can be at risk when absences and tardies grow excessive. Some schools handle this using strategies that border on the absurd, like taking attendance at 11 am instead of first thing in the morning just to increase the chances of numbers looking good.

At the individual classroom level, the frustrations associated with absence and tardiness are different. Teachers can obviously see what a concrete difference it makes to a child's curricular progress when the child misses a lot of school. It also makes a difference to the child's position in the social community of the classroom, and to the overall feel of a community. When a child is out and then comes back, the teacher has to work harder than usual to catch them up, socially as well as academically. This adds to an already complicated workload filled with so many different types of differentiation.

There are other sides to the story too, of course. First of all, I don't know many elementary age students who are in control of whether and when they leave for school. This is a really big deal! Teachers should spend more time thinking about the logistics of the morning of the typical child in their class. When Benjamin tells Colin that Colin needs to get there on time, I wonder what he expects Colin to do. Get sick less often? I wish this were under all of our control. Tell his family to get moving faster in the morning? That works in some family circumstances, but certainly not in all. Benjamin's message is so gentle and the reasoning behind it completely understandable, but it is hard to imagine where it could realistically land for Colin.

Chronic absenteeism has long been a big problem in schools, particularly schools serving large numbers of students living in poverty. The problem has grown significantly worse since the beginning of the COVID pandemic, and teachers and school districts feel desperate to resolve it. But part of the problem actually *is* a relational problem. Families need to feel a sense of trust in what is happening for their children in schools, if they are going to prioritize getting children there punctually. Even that, which is a really big deal, is far from the whole story: families need support, not punishment or strict talks. Families need better access to food, transportation, reasonable housing, heat, childcare for younger siblings, medical and dental services. Secure, steady, and strong access to any one item on that list does genuinely make it easier to get children to school.

What seems unlikely to help get a child to school is overtly telling the child that he needs to do a better job getting there. Most children already know this. All it creates for Colin here is a sense of shame, palpable in his silence and body language, a sense that his teacher wants him – and possibly also his family – to do things differently, to be different from how they are. Colin is still plenty willing to work for and learn from Benjamin, but something about their relationship is compromised in this back and forth.

Again, I do not fault Benjamin, who is trying to make it clear to Colin that he actually can do the math if he is there to learn it. I am simply offering this as another example where the roles of teacher and student pose particular challenges to this thing we call a relationship. Let's remember the real limits to children's power and control in their daily lives and find ways to support them that don't ask them to change what they cannot or feel bad about their situational disempowerment. Yes, there are resources – caregivers, guidance counselors, social workers – who might be able to help get Colin to school on time consistently, but even accessing these resources is something an adult needs to take on. Colin just doesn't have the wherewithal.

## High Expectations

Part of my job as a teacher educator is supervising student teachers and then evaluating them according to a state-mandated framework about what effective practice is. Where I live, we work with seven "essential elements." The Commonwealth of Massachusetts has determined that proficiency in these elements is what it takes for a candidate to be "ready to teach." (Intriguingly, in the seven years I have been working with this framework, the elements have already changed three times, and I hear another change is in the works.)

For now, one of the elements is High Expectations. When we observe student teachers, we are meant to look for evidence that they believe all children can learn, or "can meet... standards through effective effort rather than innate ability" (MA DESE, 2024). A teacher with high expectations "...clearly communicates high standards for student work, effort, and behavior."

This language is unique to Massachusetts, but the overall demand for high expectations is part of the overall trend, cemented decades ago by President George W. Bush's No Child Left Behind legislation, to frame socially just teaching as teaching that maintains academically rigorous standards. The thinking behind this is that when teachers adjust expectations to perceptions of student capacity, poor children, BIPOC children, and children with diagnosed disabilities are often, because of teacher and systemic bias, held to lower standards that then get reflected in their learning. A mandate to hold everyone to high standards is, according to this line of thinking, a way of improving fairness in schools.

I appreciate this way of thinking. I have seen classrooms where overly low or evidently biased expectations result in dumbing down a curriculum and damaging children's learning and self-esteem. But there are problems with high expectations, too. For one thing, they are part of a cultural turn, including concepts like "growth mindset" and "grit," that likes to imagine schoolchildren exist separately from the life circumstances they have to endure.

I do not mean that because a child is experiencing food insecurity, they cannot learn math. But surely an acknowledgment of the extra burden that child has to carry, the extra challenge between that child and efficient division of fractions, is an appropriate educational adjustment. It is one thing to tell teachers not to give into myths about "innate ability"; it is another to imply that "effective effort" is enough to erase unjust circumstances.

Another issue with asking for high expectations is the rarity of any acknowledgment of how these expectations impact relationships. Do you feel closer to someone who holds high expectations for you, or to someone who sees and accepts you for who and how you are? I think the answer to that question, for most of us, is an uncertain one – one that varies from person to person and from one situation to another. Sometimes, it feels really good to know that another person expects a lot from us. Other times, it feels like implicit, constant criticism, like never measuring up. When the latter takes hold, it is hard on a relationship! No wonder some children decide that a relationship with their teacher is not a place they care to invest too much energy.

This is what we might see happening between Benjamin and Colin. Benjamin has such friendly banter, and he is saying things that make perfect sense. Come to school, and you will learn more math. Don't come to school, and math will be harder. He is not being mean or punitive in his explanation. In fact, he repeatedly tells Colin the truth: he isn't mad. He just wants Colin to understand. I think he is successful, too – Colin does understand the main point Benjamin is making. But he also clearly feels ashamed. Maybe it is a shame that will ultimately be beneficial to his education. Certainly, that is possible, and it would be a mistake to consider that all shame in education is automatically problematic. But this shame impacts how Colin relates to Benjamin in the moment, and possibly how Colin thinks about relationships with teachers overall.

## What Colin Says

Like many of the students I interviewed, Colin was lukewarm about his relationships with his teachers in our private conversation. This happened several weeks after the episode I witnessed between Benjamin and Colin. Colin really was absent frequently, and although his family consented to his participation in my research, finding a time when he was in school and not completely occupied catching up on something he had missed proved difficult.

When I asked Colin who he felt close to in school, he shrugged. I noticed that he looked impatient with my questioning, and I asked, "Do you want to go back to the classroom?" I reminded him that spending time with me was completely optional.

"Nah," he said, kicking his foot, "This is good."

I asked Colin whether he feels like he has a good relationship with his teachers, and he thought for a moment. "I like when they do silly stuff, sing songs, dance around," he told me. "I feel good with them sometimes, yeah, when they do stuff like that."

I recognized the kinds of moments Colin was describing. Benjamin and Laila have some funny song and dance routines they fall into pretty frequently during the week, and the mood in the classroom is always calm and cheerful when this happens. I could understand why that would make Colin feel more positive toward them, and why this might enhance a sense of connection or relationship.

Colin made me think about the difference between just having a sense of liking someone and feeling okay in their presence, and having an intimate or personal connection. He likes when the classroom feels happy and good. He likes it less when his teachers get really close to him in particular. These dance parties and silly routines are times when Colin is not under a microscope. No one is asking him to try harder, learn differently, or change his family's morning routine.

I asked Colin if he could draw a picture of feeling close to someone at school, but he declined. "Do I have to?" At that point, he was obviously anxious to rejoin his class, and I thanked him for his help. It can be hard to move through school feeling like you are a bit unsatisfactory to your teachers, and it is likely to affect your understanding of closeness: of who you are, of how you are perceived, and of what the other people in your life want from you. Colin showed me that these experiences do not entirely void the possibility of connection, but they make the moments of connection less about personal encounters and more about a sense of calm, happy fun in the room.

This conversation with Colin made me remember a conversation I had long ago with Laurie, a veteran preK teacher in the elementary school where I worked. Laurie lamented that when she talks to students from decades past, she always hopes they remember particular educational experiences she planned for them: times in the block corner, field trips, collectively written stories. She also hopes they remember her moments of connecting with them: drying tears, talking about new siblings, enjoying ideas together. Instead, Laurie told me, she has learned that what her alums usually reflect on is the *feeling* in the classroom – that it was jovial and warm. Laurie found this disappointing. She craved a sense that something deeper than "just" good times was going on in her classes, and, as a fellow teacher also dedicated to profound and meaningful practice, I understood this at the time.

Now, though, and with Colin's reactions in mind, I can see how that is a wish that centers the teacher's perspective and need for gratification to the exclusion of some children's experiences. It is another kind of high expectations, another way of wanting some children to be other than who and what they are. What if what a child most wants from school is the particular alive, exciting feeling of being part of a community that can have fun together? Then it makes sense that this would be the focus of the day's experience as well as the focus of sustaining memories.

A teacher might want to feel like what the child needs and later remembers is something she, the teacher, uniquely offered, but this is not ultimately about the child. When these different kinds of desires coexist, there is going to be a bit of disappointment. That colors the relationship because neither party is there to fully give the other what they want or hope for.

## Balancing Expectations and Acceptance

My wife and I teeter between holding one another to high expectations and accepting each other for who we are all the time. A few weeks ago, she was putting away laundry and opened one of my dresser drawers. "It's a mess in here!" she said with some disgust.

I looked up from where I was reading. "You knew what you were getting into when you married me," I reminded her. She laughed. It is an ongoing, low-grade dispute between us, and at this point, nearly two decades into marriage, it really is laughable. I have no illusion that it will feel different in another twenty years! Probably I will never keep my clothes that neat, and probably, she will never stop wishing that I did.

With things like that – putting clothes away, following up on emails – in the context of a multi-year marriage, I have so far found that laughter is the best way through. But not every disjuncture among different people is laughable or loving. Sometimes relationships ask so much more of us, and sometimes, it can be more than we are willing to give. What does that mean, then, about the staying power of a relationship?

On my wedding day, my father-in-law pulled me aside. He and my mother-in-law had been married for over thirty years at that point; now, they are approaching fifty. He was uncharacteristically serious when he asked me if I wanted marriage advice from him, and I nodded. "Sure." What he said has stuck with me, "Well, there's love, of course, and that's the main thing." He laughed, sounding more like himself. "Maybe that's the only thing!"

Then he grew sober again. He said, "And the other key to success is just, don't expect the other person to change. Accept them for who they are." I waited, thinking this over, and he gestured to where his wife was vigorously sponging his breakfast crumbs off the counter. "Of course," he said, back to laughter, "Felice still hasn't learned that!"

At the time, the conversation felt surreal. I didn't yet feel comfortable with my place in their family, and that week was so overwhelmingly emotional that I couldn't process anything properly. "That's about really old people," I remember thinking. And it is – but young and old people don't seem as different to me now as they once did.

Reflecting on that conversation now, I can see that Rick was saying something powerful about uncertainty. All of these things are true at once, even as they seem mutually exclusive. A strong relationship means accepting a person for who they are, not expecting them to change. If they leave crumbs on the counter, get to school late... chances are they are going to keep leaving crumbs on the counter and getting to school late. Take it or leave it! But at the same time, closeness means expecting more from someone, holding out for just a little better for and from them, pushing them to be their best selves.

Teaching is obviously not marriage. It doesn't seem worth going into the many self-evident reasons this analogy falls short. Instead, I want to point out the lesson about uncertainty that comes from working temporarily with the connection in spite of its imperfections. Teachers are in a difficult position when it comes to showing children love, especially when we think about love as something that embeds acceptance. There is a real, contractual limit to how much a teacher can play their role or do their job properly and still accept children for who they are.

There is a limit, too, to how much teachers can love and accept students but still keep asking them to change. And with all this demand for growth and change, it is uncertain what kind of relationship is possible. It depends on many other factors, perhaps temperament most of all. There are children, like Colin, who find so much stress in being pushed to change even when the push is as reasonable as Benjamin's attempted lesson about coming to school consistently and punctually. When his teachers push him like this, especially since there is probably not much he can do about what they want from him, it is unsurprising that Colin prefers to fade into the background moments of school, when he can enjoy the pleasant atmosphere but connection and intimacy do not feel primary. I'm pleased that Colin gets to experience that joy, and at the same time, I see why it might look somehow insufficient. With these children, teachers have to walk the line between unconditional love and sponging crumbs, and it is a position of uncertainty. That is labor that deserves a name.

## When Kids Want Teachers to Change

As much as teachers want children to change, the converse is also true – anyone who has ever talked casually with a group of children about school knows that they sometimes want their teachers to change. None of the children I interviewed in either class described a wish that their teachers were different, but I have known enough children over time to understand that this is partly a function of their unwillingness to admit such a wish to an adult. My last book looked at the concept of consent in the childhood classroom, and I spent a lot of time thinking about the idea that children do not generally consent to spend their days in school. Plenty of kids like school, it is true, and many of them get a lot out of it even if they do not always like it. But compulsory schooling is not a consensual phenomenon.

One of the things I discovered as part of that project is that a lot of children go into school expecting something substantially different from what they end up getting. Some kids think their teacher is going to have a magical tool to "make them smart." Others imagine school as a place they will feel cozy, calm, and quiet, and then they are surprised by how energetic and noisy the whole thing is. Others still wish that school were all about having fun: climbing on walls, playing outrageous pranks, staying up all night with jungle animals. None of these fantasies is totally possible, and their desirability is debatable too.

The point is not that children should be able to do what they want to in school all the time. That is not how a functional community works, even though it is one particular fantasy about freedom. I tend to think many children would benefit, on balance, from *some* more opportunity to turn school into what they want it to be, but even I am aware of significant boundaries I cannot imagine wanting to see crossed. When we want to coexist ethically and meaningfully with other people, we sometimes have to compromise our impulses and desires.

But when we make those compromises or sacrifices of wish and will, it helps to spend a moment acknowledging that the sacrifice exists. I think something similar is true about how many children feel about their teachers. It is difficult for a child to admit that they want a key adult in their life to be different from how they are. This often changes dramatically in adolescence. Younger children, though, respond intensely to an expectation that they accept adults as a given, and an understanding that this acceptance is part of being "good."

It definitely makes teachers' lives and work easier when students continue the veneer of loving and accepting their teachers for exactly who they are, but I still believe many children wish their teachers would be different. Some wish their teachers were more lenient; others wish their teachers were harsher, particularly on other children who seem to be getting in the way. Is it possible that all of the children I interviewed feel somewhere on the continuum from a bit indifferent to incredibly loving toward their teachers? Certainly, but I think it is more likely on balance that they largely understood me, an adult, as allied with their teachers, and as such, they didn't want to risk sounding disrespectful or inappropriate. They also probably worried that I would report back to Ainsley, Laila, and Benjamin.

Can you remember the first time you were aware of wanting a teacher to change? Sometimes children talk about this with their friends or family. Other times, they show their frustration via a range of behaviors, or they just hold it in and wait it out. How to respond to frustrations with people who don't please us can actually be an important part of education, and I don't always think it is a bad thing for a child to need to work this out or cope with liking or loving a person while acknowledging their limitations. This happens in family relationships and friendships, too. What needs to be present in a relationship, though, for it to feel worthwhile even in the face of a strong wish for the other person to be different?

Though I cannot answer this question definitively, I again find it helpful to return to the ways the same problem works for me in other kinds of relationships. In general, I can handle someone wanting me to change if I have a sense that they know and accept the essence of me, in a deep and underlying way. But if I were pushed to define this more precisely: "How do I know that acceptance is there? How can I be sure when it is not? What even *is* the essence of me? Do I accept it myself?" I would struggle. I don't actually believe there is a certain answer to these questions, which is why acceptance can feel every bit as fuzzy as love. How do we ever know we are accepting an actual person, and not our fantasy about who the person is?

Teachers cannot change, and usually are not interested in changing, to meet the specific desires of each of their individual students, though over time, children and their needs and desires probably shape how our teaching evolves. This is especially true, and especially complicated, because teachers are rarely relating to just one student at a time. The idea that even three, much less twenty, children would want their teacher to be the same way, is unlikely. A teacher might treat children differently based on her internal assessment of what a child can handle or what they need, and this may or may not align with what the child experiences, but the teacher is unlikely to essentially change. It is another area of power unevenness in the classroom dynamic. It is also a reminder that the relationship between child and teacher, like any other relationship, asks a lot of its participants, and there may be times when what it asks is beyond the realm of the possible.

## Closing with Questions

This chapter has taken up the question of whether we can be close to someone and still want them to change, and conversely, whether we can be close to someone who wants change from us. Use these questions to push your thinking about how the themes, topics, and stories in this chapter may relate to your own practice.

- Think about some of the changes you want to see in one or more of your students. How do you think wanting to see change impacts your way of relating to them?
    *As a teacher, it is part of your job to push for change in your students: academic growth, behavior development, social and character evolution, too. When you think about the changes you hope to see, what comes to mind first? Do some students come to mind more than others? Think about how you experience, inside yourself, the hope that your students will change. How do you show or talk about this with your students? How do they know that you hope to see these changes? What are some of the ways these hopes or goals impact your relationship?*
- What are some times someone has wanted you to change in an important way? How did that affect your relationship with that person?

> *All of us have experienced the feeling of being in some kind of relationship – friendly, familial, romantic, professional – where we sensed that someone else wished we were different in a key way. When has this happened to you, and how have you become aware of it? How did it impact your relationship, but also, what does it make you think about how the wish for change affects relationships more broadly?*

- What does it feel like to you when students do not seem to be growing or changing enough, and how do you handle those feelings?

   > *Again, it is part of your job as a teacher to want growth and change from your students. But children do not often grow and change according to a teacher's wishes or schedule! How do you handle the frustration or disappointment that arises when your students are not changing the ways you wish they were, or when you realize they cannot, as with Colin getting to school on time? How do you think this impacts your relationships with them or their sense of how you feel about them?*

- What are some of the ways you think students have wished you would change? How do you handle your awareness of these wishes?

   > *Are students likely to wish you were more lenient, stricter, more organized, less enthusiastic? What do you do when you notice that a student might not love or even accept you for who you are? How do you handle that observation within yourself, and how do you handle it in the broader context of your classroom relationships?*

## References

Massachusetts Department of Elementary and Secondary Education. Guidelines for the Candidate Assessment of Performance (CAP). 2024. https://www.doe.mass.edu/edprep/cap/cap-guidelines.pdf

# 6

# Can You Be Close to Someone Who Doesn't Want to Be Close to You?

Several of the chapters you have read indicate that not all children actually want to be in a relationship with their teachers. Some, like first-grade Simone from Chapter 4, would rather be at home, cuddling with their parents on the couch – school is something that happens until they can get back there. Others, like fifth-grade Colin from Chapter 5, find it so frustrating that their teachers want nearly impossible change from them that they invest their relational energies elsewhere. For these children, school can be really fun, but it isn't about intimate connections.

Again and again, teachers are counseled by popular and scholarly educational discourse to build relationships with children, but one thing that is rarely addressed is the possibility that these relationships may feel nonconsensual to children. What are we, as adults, teaching children when we insist not only that they go to school every day, do the work we tell them to do and learn the concepts we tell them to learn, but also that they have to participate in relationships with their teachers – whether or not they want to?

The overall cultural messaging around this topic tends to fault teachers who are somehow inadequate at igniting children's interest in a relationship. Teachers are given innumerable strategies for connecting with students: greet them by name, learn about their interests, bend down to their physical level, respond to their anxieties and questions with compassion, praise them with specific language for their efforts and successes. Sometimes, these strategies "work." They make school warmer and more palatable for plenty of children, and I would never tell a teacher to stop doing these things.

What's more, there is also something about spending hours and hours together, day after day, that does result in a relationship, like it or not. There is that feeling a lot of teachers recognize after the year's first hurdles are over, when the classroom buzzes with the companionable feeling of people who are used to one another's strengths and struggles, more or less understand what to expect, and at least tolerate each other's company. That feeling is, I think, what some teachers are referencing when they compare a classroom community to a family, and I know how sustaining and enlivening it can be.

So there clearly are plenty of reasons that relationships in school can be adaptive, appealing, and genuinely beneficial – to probably most teachers, and to *some* students. But why is it required? What does the mandate show those children who would rather not think about their teachers in those terms? What does it mean to use the language of relationships to talk about something that, for some, is functional, compulsory, and tolerable at best? This chapter examines whether it is possible or appropriate to be close to someone who doesn't want to be close to you.

## Andrea Can't Stop Laughing

Andrea, a white girl, is one of the more overtly confident students in Ainsley's class. She is already a strong reader and writer, and it seems that her peers like her, seeking her out for help and companionship. Ainsley also often calls on her to assist with difficult tasks. The first time I met Andrea, she struck me as happy and collected, mature, and at ease in the company of other children as well as adults.

During classroom observations, I also noticed that Andrea had a strong connection to Ainsley. Every time she comes to the classroom, she runs up to Ainsley and greets her effusively, usually with a giant grin. I have seen Andrea jump out of her other classroom – which, in Ainsley's school, is Andrea's "home base"– and run up to Ainsley for a quick hug before bounding back. When Ainsley asks Andrea to do something challenging, whether academic or social, Andrea always seems eager to engage. In fact, the connection between Andrea and Ainsley stood out to me as a notably strong one, similar to other relationships I see develop between teachers and students who both have energetic, positive, and buoyant personalities.

Because of this, I expected Andrea's interview to be one of the many where Ainsley's students described how much they love their teacher and how loved Ainsley makes them feel. I predicted that Andrea would be as eager to describe her sense of closeness with Ainsley as she was eager to satisfy her teacher's requests in class. Our interview started easily, and Andrea was openly curious about my project.

After we spoke for a few minutes, and I explained to her that I was exploring relationships and closeness, especially between children and their teachers, I asked Andrea who she feels close to in school. To my surprise, she grew very quiet and thought for quite a while before answering. "I think I mostly feel close to my friends," she eventually said, before listing the names of several other girls in her grade. I asked her why, and she thought again. "We have a lot of fun together, they're very fun to be with."

Next, I asked Andrea directly if she feels close to any of her teachers. "What?" she asked. I repeated the question. "What?" she said again, but this time, it was not the "what" of someone who hadn't heard but, rather, of someone who finds the question preposterous. Then, Andrea started to laugh. I smiled, a little perplexed but also taken by her energy, and asked, "Does that seem funny to you?" Andrea didn't answer; instead she just kept laughing. Her laughing got louder and more raucous. I said, "I guess my question must seem pretty silly." She nodded, "Yeah, it really does," she agreed, still laughing, "It does! I love my teachers and they teach me so GOOD! But my friends, my friends are the ones I feel close to."

Andrea was brave, confident, and also unusual in her willingness to laugh overtly at my suggestion, but I'm not sure how unusual she was in finding the suggestion ridiculous. As previous chapters have discussed, plenty of other children also consider closeness something to aspire to with friends, but not with teachers. This isn't to say, though, that all or any of these children feel hostile toward their teachers. Andrea likes Ainsley, even using the word "love" to describe how she feels about teachers in general. She never seems anything but happy and secure in Ainsley's presence.

When children edge away from relationships with their teachers, it doesn't mean their teachers are doing anything wrong! It might mean that while some children long for close relationships with their teachers, that isn't true for all of them. Ultimately, this is true about so many different kinds of connections. Some colleagues want work friendships; others want to maintain a boundary. My wife describes patients who really want to connect with her as a physician and others who are perfectly polite but would rather just get refills and basic preventive care. Imagine if your doctor, your cousin, or your boss *insisted* that you feel some kind of emotional closeness. Sometimes, wouldn't that just make you want to draw a stronger boundary – either that or, like Andrea, burst into laughter?

What do some children's relational boundaries, conscious or inadvertent, mean about their teachers' constant efforts to build those relationships? Is it the job of the teacher to somehow inspire the child to *want* to have a closer connection? Some teachers and many classroom management experts do seem to think this is the case. I also think it's usually nice to see teachers trying, but trying too hard, *pushing* a connection, is a practice we would frown upon in almost any other kind of relationship. I am not sure where the right line is, and it seems to me another area where certainty is a pretense. Andrea is confident about recognizing the silliness of the idea for herself, though. Most children are less sure than her, which, to my mind, makes the question an even bigger one.

## Two Sides to the Story

Ainsley is an incredibly loving, patient teacher, and, like all teachers and all humans, she also has days when she struggles. For her, this comes out in a cycle of feeling really down about herself, questioning whether she is making any difference as a teacher, lashing out slightly at her students in fatigue and frustration, and then experiencing guilt because she lashed out.

I saw Ainsley go through this cycle several times during our work together, and it is a familiar cycle to me – probably to many teachers. If my portrayal of her so far in this book is overall rosy, it is because I think she is generally a fantastic teacher – I'd be thrilled to have my children in her class – and also because I am aware of the effort she puts in to keep the struggles at bay. I also wouldn't want any reader to think, though, that Ainsley's emotional landscape is completely even, or that she never loses her temper with her students.

The angriest I ever heard Ainsley get at her students happened soon after the winter break, when it was cold and the days were still short. She confided to me that the children were having a harder time than she had expected getting back into the routines of the day, and that the lack of outdoor playtime was also impacting their behavior.

Ainsley was also feeling stressed out because she was responsible for completing individual benchmark reading assessments for all children in the grade. Many of the children weren't performing as well as she had hoped, and this made her anxious about her teaching quality, even though she knew on some level that the assessment wasn't particularly meaningful. She was also having some winter blues of her own and felt like the next vacation was just too far away. Before I came in to observe Ainsley warned me, "Things have been a little chaotic!"

*I get to Ainsley's room expecting chaos because of her warning, and am surprised instead to find the children sitting quietly at their desks, working hard to write sentences on white boards. Ainsley is holding up large, laminated cards with words on them, one at a time. The children are meant to write one sentence using each of the words she holds up. The work is slow and laborious, and the noise level in the room keeps rising.*

*As often happens when I observe whole groups of students at work, I notice how different the room looks and feels depending on who I am looking at and who I am thinking about the most. If I focus on Ainsley, I see her holding the cards and trying hard to keep children's attention. She holds up the word, "she." The students pronounce the word and spell it out chorally with Ainsley, "S, H, E," and then they copy it onto their white boards. She instructs, "Okay, now think of a sentence with 'she' in it. Turn to your neighbor and say your sentence!"*

*The children turn toward one another and start sharing sentences. Immediately the room grows very loud. "Boys and girls!" Ainsley says, "You're sharing your sentences, but you're doing it quietly!"*

*This is when I start thinking about the story from the perspective of BJ, who is sitting near me. BJ has written an S and part of an H, and he eagerly pronounced "she" with his classmates, but he can't write quickly enough, or focus intently enough, to finish the first thing his teacher asked him to do. He lights up noticeably when she says to turn to his neighbor, leaning over and immediately launching into a loud soliloquy about the video game he was playing this morning on the bus.*

*When Ainsley says, "...you're doing it quietly," BJ looks befuddled. How can he talk, but also be quiet? He sits back down and puts his head on his white board, then again looks startled when he notices that part of the "s" has rubbed onto his forehead. Obviously I'm not inside his mind, but I become so aware of how the classroom is existing in all these different ways at once, how there are so many different stories unfolding. Maybe this is what Ainsley tried to encapsulate by using the word "chaotic."*

*Things get a little softer again as some children give up and others whisper with their neighbors about sentences including "she." Ainsley goes to kneel before Finley, who is still copying the word, tracing her own letters again and again, meticulous. "Finley," Ainsley asks, "Can you think of a sentence for she?"*

*"Ummmmm," Finley responds, "Ummmm…"*

*Ainsley puts one hand on Finley's shoulder. "Can you look up at me while we are talking about this?"*

*Finley stops writing and looks up. "Ummmm…" she says again. The ambient noise in the room has risen again, and Ainsley stands up. "It is TOO LOUD in here!" she says. While she is standing, Finley looks back down at her white board. She uses her white board marker to gently poke Carissa, next to her, and both girls start to giggle.*

*"Boys and girls," Ainsley continues, "I am feeling frustrated. Frustrated and… I am getting really ANNOYED!" When she says annoyed, her pitch goes up, and the room grows nearly silent. Ainsley almost never raises her voice, so it is cause for great interest and, in some cases, concern from the children. Because I know Ainsley well by now, I know that later she will be deeply upset with herself for even this level of outburst. She takes a breath and looks back at me; I smile and hope that brings her some comfort and confidence.*

*Without saying anything else to the rest of the class, Ainsley crouches down beside Finley again and notes that Finley has now dropped her marker. "Finley!" Ainsley says, "I know this is hard, I really know this is hard, hard work, but I know you, and I know you can do it. Let's really focus now, let's think of a sentence for 'she.'" Before they get very far, though, Ainsley has to rise again to quiet the room.*

From the vantage point of paying attention to teachers and teaching, this vignette looks like a story about Ainsley's frustration and the class' lack of responsiveness to her. Though the children quiet down every time she tells them to, the quiet never lasts long, and few children get their sentences written.

Even in the midst of this somewhat stressful lesson, Ainsley is also using some of her signature strategies to try to relate intimately to Finley. She gets down to Finley's physical level, pushes for eye contact, and talks to her directly. When Finley hesitates, she offers encouragement and confidence as well as empathy for the hard work Finley is doing.

Just as looking at BJ altered my perspective in the moment, though, when I read back over my notes and tried to consider the episode from Finley's point of view, the entire scene read differently. Since I know I can't really understand how Finley is perceiving things, I won't try to write this through a child's voice – this is merely a slightly altered retelling of the same vignette, but trying to center a child's perspective – particularly a child who is more interested in other things besides forming a relationship with her teacher.

*Ainsley is telling the class to write sentences that have particular words in them, and it is hard to think of sentences for some of these words. "She" is a word with endless possible sentences, but also, when you are seven years old, "she" isn't necessarily a word that seems to mean all that much. Writing it carefully, with letters you only started learning a year ago, is plenty of work in and of itself. Many of the children in the class seem to believe that following Ainsley's directions is what will make them a better writer, and they want to be better writers. But following her directions is also hard to do, and there are plenty of other things going on.*

*Every once in a while, Ainsley tells them that instead of writing, they should stop and talk to the person next to them. This is a more appealing instruction. Finley is sitting next to Carissa, a girl she is not close friends with but really likes and admires. She thinks Carissa is nice and funny, she has the same backpack as Carissa, and she wants Carissa to like her, too. So it is kind of exciting to have a chance to talk to her, to work on their relationship.*

*The problem is, they are supposed to be saying sentences to one another, and Carissa is looking at Lyuba and Jack, who are sitting across* from her in their desk group. Finley knows Carissa and Lyuba are close, because they play together at recess just about every day. Finley is trying to think of a sentence that might get Carissa's attention away from Lyuba, all to herself. Then, while she is working on this, Ainsley comes over to help her.

Finley wants to please Ainsley, partly because she likes her but also because she understands that you are supposed to make your teacher happy. In general, she knows that adults, like her mom and stepfather, like it when other adults, such as her teacher, are also happy with her. She also knows that doing the thing the teacher wants you to do seems like the best way to make the teacher happy. But she is distracted by wanting Carissa's attention and how noisy the room is around her, and anyway, she can't think of a sentence. She can't even necessarily remember what the sentence is supposed to be about, or what a sentence is. Also, it is frustrating to have to work with the teacher exactly when everyone else is getting a chance to just talk with their friends.

Luckily, everyone else's talking gets Ainsley's attention away, and Finley uses the opportunity to poke Carissa with her marker cap, right in her arm. This gets Carissa's notice, and that makes Finley happy, even if she accidentally drops her marker in the process.

Of course, exactly what Finley is doing in this scenario is speculative, though I spent enough time watching and talking with her to understand how much she wants to connect with Carissa and some of the other more evidently popular girls in her class. The point is that at any given moment, children and teachers aren't consistently working toward the same purposes, and a classroom encounter can look incredibly maddening or very productive depending on the vantage point we take.

For Finley, Ainsley's efforts to build and also capitalize on their relationship during this class period are somewhere between meaningless and frustrating, because they get in the way of a peer relationship she is more interested in. It isn't that she doesn't like Ainsley or care about pleasing her. It's just that her relationship with her teacher is not as high a priority for her as some of the other relationships in her world.

Similarly, BJ is looking for the moments in the lesson when he can talk to his neighbor about the video game that he spends a lot of energy thinking about. Ainsley's emotional expressions – her pleasure, her frustration – these feel almost incidental to BJ, things that are happening as he engages with his whiteboard, his peers, his own body. He is plenty busy, though, and learning, like Finley is – just, neither of them is learning what Ainsley has set out to teach. They don't want to connect with her, at least not today, no matter how or what she tries. She does keep trying, though, and it stands out that sometimes, Ainsley's efforts at not just teaching but deeply connecting can be experienced by some children as an imposition.

## You're Not the Only Ones in the Room

I often observed similar dynamics in Benjamin and Laila's classroom when they grew frustrated with their students. This observation happened during early spring, when Laila was teaching reading comprehension groups and Benjamin was doing spelling exercises with pairs of children.

By this time of the year, fifth graders were growing anxious about their approaching graduation and transition to middle school. For many of them, this would mean not only saying goodbye to this year's teachers, but also, because of the ways the middle schools in the district were zoned, separating from peers they'd been in school with since preK. Conversations about what to expect in middle school were also becoming more frequent, and Laila and Benjamin were both feeling anxious about whether their students were "ready" for the academic and social challenges that lay ahead. In the midst of this anxiety, I noticed both teachers were a little less patient than usual with their students.

*Honorah, Eleanor, Javier, and Birdy are working with Laila on questions about a story they read together last week. Someone from the school cafeteria enters the room with small bags of apple slices.*

Laila looks up, "Oh, thank you!" She looks at Benjamin, "I guess snack is a little early today."

Benjamin puts his finger up to indicate that he wants to finish what he is doing. Laila turns back to her group; the cafeteria worker puts a tray with apple bags on top of a bookshelf and leaves. "There's apples now," Birdy says.

"Yeah," Laila says, "We'll pass them out in a few minutes."

"I'm not that hungry yet," mentions Eleanor, poking Birdy, "Are you?"

Birdy shrugs, "No, I don't really like those apples anyway. They taste like soap."

"They do!" says Eleanor, "They DO taste like soap, that's just what they taste like!" Without meaning to, I laugh – I wouldn't have used those words, but now that Birdy has pointed it out, I know exactly what she means about those pre-sliced apple baggies. Unfortunately, my laughter eggs them on, and they start giggling more wildly.

"Girls," says Laila, and points down at the questions they are discussing.

Just then, Chris, who is playing Lexia on his Chromebook across the room, gets up. "Apples!" he says, and saunters over to the apple tray. "It's apples for snack," he says, sounding glum.

"Birdy says they taste like soap," Eleanor tells Chris. He laughs.

"Chris," Laila says, and points back to his Chromebook, "We'll do apples in a minute. Now it's time for Lexia."

"Like SOAP," Chris laughs, and comes to stand next to Birdy, "School apples DO taste like soap."

"Chris!" Laila repeats, "Girls, you were doing so well with your questions, What do you think is going to happen to the characters in the next chapter? Are they making good choices?"

"They're making soap choices," Birdy says, and looks right at Chris. They both start to laugh together. Eleanor soon joins the laughter, "Soap apples are like soaples!" she says. All three children are laughing now.

"I'm feeling really frustrated," Laila says, "I told you we'll have snack in a little while. Come on, you three, let's really try to stay focused. Remember: you're not the only ones in the room."

Like the vignette from Ainsley's classroom, this one looks so different, relationally, depending on the perspective you take. Laila feels frustrated because her students are growing distracted by their snack and aren't listening to her. She is using a lot of the kinds of strong relational tactics popular literature advises teachers to use: she keeps her voice calm, affirms the children's feelings (like the fact that they are probably hungry), and praises the hard work they have been doing up until the apple incident. She corrects the children's behavior without chastising or humiliating them. When her initial efforts fail, she models using words to describe her feelings of frustration and also invoke what these three children owe the rest of the community.

For Birdy, Chris, and Eleanor, the story is one about laughing together and cementing social relationships. It is also a story about how strange the world of school can be. Why do American institutions feed children pre-sliced apples in sealed plastic bags? Why do we put food in front of children but tell them to wait until the scheduled time to eat? We should not expect children to consider that normal or acceptable. That they find community in laughing at the absurdity heartens me. If doing so means showing Laila they don't want what she has to offer at that moment – not her apples and not her instruction – then maybe it's worthwhile.

Birdy, Eleanor, and Chris aren't usually friends. Birdy and Eleanor often work together because they are similarly strong readers, but they are in different social groups within Laila and Benjamin's classroom. This was the only time in all of my observations that I saw Chris have anything to do with either of them, and Laila later confirmed my assessment, "He usually hangs out with other boys, and they're almost always talking about sports." For these three, this is a brief story about relationship building, but it is not about the relationship between students and teachers. In fact, Laila comes off as somewhat irritating, in the way of what feels like it matters to them most. Their laughter, their collaborative distraction, their disgust at the "soaples," these are the relational priorities of the episode for the children who are in it.

## All Kids Want a Connection

Thinking about the ways some children prioritize relationships with one another, or with their own inner worlds, over relationships with teachers, I started noticing more and more of these scenes: episodes where Ainsley, Benjamin, and Laila grew frustrated with children's behavior and low-grade but evident disinterest in engaging in deep relationships with them. A similar pattern unfolded each time: children were interested in relating to one another, and the ways they pursued these relationships appeared silly and distracting to the teacher. The teacher responded by going increasingly into what Ainsley would call "teacher mode," chastising the children gently while also drawing on specific tools oriented toward garnering compliance. Children responded to this move differently, depending on temperament, specifics of circumstance, and innumerable other factors, but the end result was usually a sense of a slight chasm between some children and the teacher.

I started to notice this pattern so often that I decided to speak with the teachers about it. One day, when I was talking to Ainsley, I asked, "What do you do when children don't want to have a relationship with you? What happens when, in a particular moment, it seems like children are just interested in other things besides connecting with you, their teacher?"

Ainsley replied by reminding me of a theme she had spoken about before. "I used to take it really personally," she said, "because of how much I needed to heal from some other things in my life. But I understand it better now, I know it's not really about rejection."

"What do you think it is about?" I asked her, agreeing that rejection isn't really the framework for considering these situations.

> Well, I think sometimes if kids are having hard times like that... those conflicts... I remind myself they're not

from me. The conflicts are about other issues. The kids all need me and they need consistency in their lives. They have big emotions but they always want love and all children need a connection. They might be having a tough day with me but then they are going home and once they get there, they feel like they actually had the best time with me. That's why I always remind them… I say, even though I am kind of harsh with you, I am doing it because you're loved.

All of the things Ainsley says here have truth to them. A day can feel incredibly tough to teachers and children when they are living through it, and feel vastly different – like a lot of fun, like a really important transformation – with some time and space to reflect. Ainsley *does* constantly remind her students how loved they are, and it is difficult to imagine anyone in her class ever doubting the authenticity of that love. She says it in words, and she also shows it in her consistency, her smiles, her warm demeanor, and her willingness to go the extra mile.

I question the part of what Ainsley is saying about whether all children need a connection to the teacher. Certainly a lot of children need that connection a lot of the time, but increasingly through my observations, I wondered if the connections children were really seeking out in a lot of their classroom behavior were connections to one another or to thoughts, playful understandings, and complex feelings inside themselves. The teacher, sometimes even by definition, is an obstacle to cementing those connections, but that is obviously hard for a teacher to acknowledge. Few of us want to be obstacles.

I asked Ainsley how she knows that all children need the connection she described. She reflected,

I needed a lot of love as a child. So maybe I'm hugging them, maybe I'm showing interest, compassion when they're having hard days… they can have a hard time understanding what love is, and some of them don't hear it a lot. Love can be hard for a six-year-old to define, but they can understand care.

For Ainsley, a student even *seeming* not to want a connection to the teacher is symptomatic of some other gap in the child's life, specifically in the kinds of love they have experienced. "I check in with them," she told me,

> if I notice their demeanor is off. And if you respect what they need to be ready, they're so much more… independent in then starting on the academic piece. Like me, if I wake up and I'm grumpy and I haven't had my coffee, it might take me a lot longer. So I think about coffee to me, as me to them. We have a longer morning routine (than in some other classrooms), and I've shown that it gives us longer learning time because I'm not continuously stopping and trying to redirect. To get ready, feel calm, and at ease… feeling safe… I really respect that if someone is irritating them, listening to what they have to say.

Ainsley shows so much empathy here, so much interest in helping children feel like they are all right emotionally as they move into and then through their school day. She expresses how deeply she cares about what is going on with children and how much she is willing to do to help them achieve equilibrium. These philosophies are a huge part of why so many of Ainsley's students feel confident in her love for them, and they are also a part of why the class is able to have a lot of fun together most of the time.

But what Ainsley is unwilling to consider is the possibility that sometimes, a child's demeanor might be off not because of something going wrong on the bus or at home, but because they would rather not be participating in the relationship. Ainsley is gifted at reading so many of her students' emotional communications, but she refuses to acknowledge or engage with the one where children are implying "just leave me alone."

Benjamin and Laila had surprisingly similar things to say about children who avoid relationships. "Some of these kids have had a really tough time," Benjamin explained.

> There might be one reason, there might be a different one. Sometimes it helps me to know the story but a lot of times, it doesn't. What you have to tell yourself is, okay, this kid is having a hard time. This isn't about me, but they need something FROM me right now, like a connection, they need to know I'm with them, I'm paying attention to them. So when I start to get frustrated, that's what I remember.

Benjamin, who is so different from Ainsley in temperament, experience, and teaching style, practically echoes her language here, including her absolute certainty that every child is seeking a connection with their teacher, and when they seem not to, it indicates some other struggle they are going through rather than a genuine disinterest.

Laila reflected in a related way. "Sometimes I take it personally," she confided, as though this were a big flaw in her attitude toward teaching instead of a nearly universal human tendency,

> but obviously I try not to, and that gets easier as I go. I just remind myself they have a lot going on. So if they seem distant one day, or if they seem distant just a lot, I try to take a deep breath and tell myself, this kid has a lot going on. A lot of times, eventually I learn… from them, or from their families… and then it kind of makes sense.

Again, I know what Laila means. There are times, maybe even for all of us, when the reason we do not lean into a connection is less because we do not want it and more because something else is preventing us from the kind of vulnerability or relaxation that intimacy requires. Some children are hesitant to build relationships with their teachers because of other relationships where things are going wrong, or because of an excess of trauma or stress in their lives. On the other hand, surely it is also possible that some children are not interested in entering into those relationships simply because they do not want to – and the assumption that this represents something "wrong" borders on the offensive. What if every time we as adults made moves to avoid a particular connection, someone assumed it was a sign of something wrong in our lives? That assumption takes away our agency, our right to decide who we want to be close to and when.

I am reminded of a casual friendship in my neighborhood. I met my neighbor at a children's swimming lesson, and we had some nice conversations. I liked her fine, but I wasn't interested in becoming close. She reached out several times to include me in potlucks and go on walks, and, out of busyness and mild disinterest, I tried to politely decline. After a few months, she stopped reaching out, and I felt a little rude but also relieved. I know, at this point in my life, that I don't have to be everyone's best friend.

Then, I ran into my neighbor at the farm share. We made pleasant conversation as we chose our heads of kohlrabi, and then she leaned in close. "Is everything okay?" she wondered. "When you stopped wanting to get together, I wondered if something was wrong, or if your family was sick." I was flummoxed and felt a bit gaslit, a feeling that morphed into more basic irritation. First, I wondered, as many children might in this position – wait, *is* something wrong? Is something wrong in my life, or with me? Then, I thought, did I really hurt her feelings? I still feel a bit guilty over that, to be honest, but the experience also reminded me how strange it feels to be pathologized for making a decision not to get close, and for someone else's feelings about that decision to be projected back onto me.

School is a lot harder than a neighborhood when it comes to gently bowing away from intimacy. Children have to negotiate these feelings and experiences with one another all day every day, often for years on end. Most of the time, when it comes to relationships that start in school, they can't decide to just stop answering texts or gently turn down invitations. They can't say outright, "I'm not interested in this relationship," and often, they can't politely turn and walk away. The only recourse they have is through their behavior, so they figure out how to build walls and achieve the distance and boundaries they need in tone and actions. Certainly, the impact can be hurtful and feel like rejection to teachers, but it is hard to know what else a child is supposed to do when they just, in my daughter's teenage terminology, aren't feeling it.

What are your internal reactions when you think about students who seem reluctant to form a strong relationship with you? Perhaps, like Ainsley, Benjamin, and Laila, you interpret these situations as signals that something negative is going on for the child, communications that mean they need you to try harder or even that they need some particular kind of help. I invite you to consider the possibility that sometimes, the desire for closeness and connection are more teacher-centered than indicative of what children consistently need. What would it mean for you to teach without being sure that your students want to connect to you? For me, this raises a lot of insecurity, but I also have to acknowledge that it is *my* insecurity, and not necessarily that of anyone else.

When teachers feel like building a relationship with every child is part of what makes us good teachers, the pressure is on. Further, many teachers want these relationships for their own sake. They gratify something, they are fun, and being loved can feel awfully good. For plenty of children, teachers' interpretations and intense efforts at closeness are helpful and enriching. They make school easier. For other children, they are undesirable. When we take that lack of desire as a sign that something is wrong with the child, we may be missing an opportunity to understand more about who they are and what they want out of the world. Sometimes, they just want to be alone, and even though that can appear alarming or confusing, it is also worthy of respect. Other times, children want to focus their energies on connecting more strongly with peers. Are they under some obligation to respond relationally to their teachers? Teachers might think carefully about requesting relational closeness from those children who communicate, time and again, that they have no interest in being close to us.

## Closing with Questions

At some point, most of us have felt a desire to get more distance from someone who is seeking us out in a relationship. Most of us have probably been on the other side of the equation, too. The questions here are designed to help you think about the themes from this chapter in connection with your own teaching practice.

- What are some times that you have felt uncertain about what a student wants from you? How do you handle that uncertainty?

    *As a teacher, it can be incredibly difficult to figure out the many ways our students are different from one another, including the ways they might want different things from us. Sometimes, you will encounter children who are hard to read. Think about a child whose relational style has seemed mysterious to you. What have you decided internally about that child, and how has it impacted your way of working with them? What might be a different perspective on the same situation, and how would taking that perspective impact or change your teaching?*

- How do your students show you whether they do or do not want to make a connection? How is this like or unlike the students you read about in this chapter?

    *Think about some of the children in the scenarios in this book who seem to be signaling to Ainsley, Benjamin, and Laila that they might prefer to be left alone or to be left to focus on relationships with friends instead of their teacher. Are there times that you have felt similar messages from your students? How do you think students tend to show you when they are not interested, and how does that lead you both to think about that student, and to respond in the moment? What do you do with feelings of uncertainty about a student's interest in a relationship with you?*

- Do you believe teachers are responsible for forming relationships with all of their students? Is there a difference between offering a relationship and pursuing one more actively and insistently? Why or why not?

    *One thing this chapter discusses is the uncertainty of forming a relationship with someone else who may not be interested, or who may not put any energy into the relationship. Ainsley, Benjamin, and Laila think that it is still the teacher's responsibility to do all they can to develop a relationship with every single child. Do you agree with this perspective? If you do, think about what it is about the nature of teaching (or of childhood) that makes this obligation true when it isn't in all other contexts. If you disagree, then see if you can formulate an argument about how teachers know whether and when to invest emotional labor in a relationship with one child or another.*

- What are some times that something has unfolded in your classroom that seems one way to you, but might look quite different from a child's perspective? How, if at all, does it affect your teaching to think about these scenarios from different angles?

    *I showed in this chapter how there are so many different ways to interpret most things that unfold in a classroom. As teachers, we are generally oriented to see things from a particular, adult point of view. There is logic to this, but it is also helpful to think about how the same event, especially when it seems like a difficult one, looks from the vantage point of one or more of its child participants. If you try to do this, how does it change the ways you think about teaching and about your relationships with the children in your class? How does it make you think differently about who and what these children are interested in? If you think it is worth building opportunities to see scenarios from multiple perspectives into your regular reflection, try to make a plan for doing so.*

# 7

# Can You Be Close to Someone When It Feels Like the World Is Ending?

Being a teacher is really, really hard. Maybe being a child is even harder. In fact, one of my sisters responds to a lot of life's struggles by simply saying, "HTBAP," or "hard to be a person." We joke that this will end up on our tombstones one day. Being a person *is* hard, and acknowledging this with someone else is part of what closeness is about, but acknowledging it doesn't always make things easier.

I am not interested in subscribing to some ideal about the ways life used to be simpler. Statements like that ignore the ways modern technologies, even with their many pitfalls, make room for leisure and freedom of thought that could not exist without them. They ignore the benefits for longevity and quality of life we can find from contemporary medicine. Perhaps most importantly, they ignore the way struggles for social justice, never complete and often nonlinear, have improved conditions for many people – including many children and teachers – since those so-called simpler times.

So yes: various aspects of contemporary life are more comfortable and even, in some particular ways, more just than they have been at different points throughout the past. Yet it is undeniable that teachers and children, both globally and specifically in a US context, are now also faced with painful social struggles and upheaval. Messaging about these struggles and upheaval is constant, vivid, and unavoidable.

Children of all ages know about school shootings and racist police brutality. They know about climate change: how every summer gets a little harder for their asthmatic friends to breathe, how school closures because of climate catastrophe weren't a thing when their parents were younger, how hurricanes and fires cause sudden school closures and previously unbelievable environmental stress in increasing numbers of US communities. Children know, often firsthand, about poverty, food insecurity, housing insecurity, and opioid epidemics. What's more, they know the ways these abstract concepts play out in particular lives: how they make sleeping impossible, parents unavailable, hunger pangs acute. Children know about economic changes related to AI. They know about screen addiction, misinformation, violent social discourse, conspiracy theories, and global pandemics. They know about political polarization, and they often know more than a lot of adults think they do about the stress we feel around all of these issues.

Of course, teachers are aware of these dynamics, too. Merely because teachers are people, we are likely to experience some kind of firsthand impact because of stress, change, and pain in the world around us. Teachers also see how these issues impact the daily world of school. It is hard to open a news site or even a web browser without reading something about how much pain children are in: hunger, mental illness, health struggles related to climate change. I have seen countless teachers struggle to find ways to shoulder these emotional burdens, even apart from the grind of regular teaching life. It is hard, so hard, to see children suffering and understand how many factors are at play but not be able to do more than the minimum about it. Teachers can feel like middle management, standing in between children and a world that hurts them, but with little recourse for making concrete change.

It is hard, too, to bear so much brunt of these stressors: children's aggression and sullenness because things really don't feel okay; parental anxiety and pressure over how to present a certain topic or how best to support and teach a child. When a child is emotionally dysregulated because the parent struggles with addiction, the teacher is often able to empathize with the child, but empathy, as far as it does go, does not always make oppositional behavior easier to bear. This is particularly true when it is coming from twenty children at once, as I know some teachers sometimes feel they are experiencing.

My friends, my sisters, my close people and I – when we feel overwhelmed, we sometimes joke, "Oh well, the world is ending anyway." "Joke" is the wrong word, though. There's nothing funny about that and it doesn't really help, except in this vague way of putting trifling concerns into a broader perspective. What I've thought about recently is that we didn't use to joke that way at all. We would say other things to generate the same perspective, but that idea that the world is ending? That only came into parlance in my adulthood. Mostly, it comes from changes in our understanding of the climate catastrophes we are slowly and sadly growing used to. For me, they are also related to a sense, as an American, that struggles for justice I care about have rocked backwards and halted – this awareness that I am witnessing people's lives getting worse instead of better.

I am revisiting this chapter in January of 2025, about a week after Donald Trump's second inauguration. To me, and to many of the families, teachers, and teacher educators I know, this month represents the beginning of an especially uncertain, even terrifying time. Teachers are receiving conflicting directives from states and districts about how to respond to potential ICE raids in their schools. Families are navigating the possibility that the government will not recognize their children's gender identities or claims to bodily autonomy. Tech moguls seem to have a new stranglehold on state policies and surveillance, and no one is sure what this will mean for children moving forward. Moreover, environmental regulations and public health safeguards, already weak, are being repealed in real time. How does a teacher, a parent, face a child, knowing this is how we are manipulating their futures?

At the same time, I also know and ultimately hope that not every reader will agree with me about the dangers inherent to this moment. That, too, raises questions about relationships: in earlier chapters, I discussed both holding onto myself and considering intense differences when pursuing and sustaining closeness. In this particularly politically fraught and polarized moment, how does a teacher face a child knowing the stakes involved in political disagreements, either between teacher and child or between teacher and family? The classroom has never existed in a vacuum from local, national, and global politics, nor should it. But given the gravity of the decisions the country and world are facing at this historical juncture, it is also important to think about the ways the encroachment of world pain – political, economic, and ecological anxieties – impact relationships between children and their teachers.

In the months between Trump's election and his inauguration, I read a lot of different kinds of articles, and listened to a lot of podcasts, about how left-leaning folks should cope with this presidency. One of the ideas I kept seeing was that clustering in small, meaningful caring communities – churches, knitting circles, book clubs – can be a form of resistance against oligarchy and fascism. The line of reasoning went something like this: in contrast to the first Trump presidency, this one exists with fewer built-in political guardrails, and there is also less momentum for outright protest. Battles are being waged in courts and in Congress, but another way to keep the world looking how we might want it to look is, quite simply, to be nice to ourselves and the people we care about. Constructing and sustaining small communities of warmth and mutual regard is in that sense an act of world building, a political act.

To be honest, at first, I thought this sounded bogus. I still kind of do. In the face of what I see as bombastic layers of oppression, censorship, and tyranny, we're supposed to… just knit sweaters and be nice? It feels both cheap and cheapening.

As I thought about it more, though, I came to understand that my reaction was partly based on the same anxieties about closeness, its possibilities, its limits, and its power that underlie this book. (I maintain, though, that my reaction actually is partly because of the feeling that such efforts don't hold a candle to what they are up against.) Maybe close relationships can function as resistance, precisely because of their capacity to become institutional structures in and of themselves: structures that remind us of warmth, of human connection, of seeing past some differences and respecting others' limits. Maybe this is the lesson that artists and writers working in other times of political terror have shown. Maybe teachers and children have, too.

At the same time, I know for sure this can be too much to ask of teachers and children, perhaps of all communities. Considering all the responsibilities America already assigns the institution of school, it would be too much to add, "coping gracefully with global pain and trauma." What does it feel like to be a child growing up with dramatic ideas in the ether around the purpose of human (and digital) institutions, the potential future of the natural world, the nature of disagreement in a democracy, even the fragility of that democracy? When teachers relate to children in schools today, this is the context. I feel that it is a lot to ask of children to trust any adults in these circumstances.

A related set of questions has to do with mental well-being and loneliness, or alienation, in modern life. There has been much attention paid in research lately to how many more people feel lonely than did ten or twenty years ago. There are lots of different reasons for this, and the most obvious and most commonly indicated culprit is the massive amount of technology in so many of our lives. The ways children interface with technology may at surface feel unrelated to concerns about climate, violence, and democracy, but actually, they are intertwined. They fall under this broader heading of the ways children have to negotiate a world that not only looks different from the one their trusted adults knew as children, but also different from one where adults can usefully offer a roadmap. Of course there is the caveat that each generation faces a different world from that of their parents, and that it can be too easy to cry "crisis." I honor this caveat and still think children today, especially in a ricocheting United States, face a particularly unstable moment.

The influx of technology, including particularly the rapidly growing role of AI and the mental health impacts of social media and screen addiction, is one more way that the human world can sometimes seem to be teetering on a scary brink. What's more, too few adults are thinking about the ways tech has changed a child's day in school, and how it might be influencing children's ways of thinking about what a teacher even is. In connection with the speedily evolving role of technology along with a changing world, I want to contemplate how children in schools are also dealing with the paradox of being close to people but still feeling lonely and isolated. It is, as my sister says, hard to be a person, but loneliness, as distinct from independence and solitude, can make it harder.

## What About Hope?

A few years ago, during the very beginning of the COVID-19 pandemic, a close mentor, Jonathan Silin, and I were giving a talk about the histories and futures of childhood. Someone in our audience asked us, what about hope? Is there a place for hope when we face children? My mentor, who has several decades on me, said that he finds hope very difficult but he also thinks anyone working with children has to find it. We can define it differently, but we can't relate to children, really look them in the eye, if we are actually hopeless.

This was a strong moral claim for him, based on the idea that to ask children to trust adults, adults have to have some sense of a future potential for those children. It was a complex moment for our audience of early childhood teachers to take in this idea. Many were managing remote work for the first time, and many feared for their health and even lives. The world felt confusing and the sudden changes facing schools felt shocking. I saw the faces on the Zoom screen register Jonathan's statement as meaningful and true, but difficult.

Then I saw an interesting thing happen: teachers, reminded of their obligation to stay with hope, started to feel more hopeful. In the conversation that followed, the teachers were able to de-center their own anxieties and quite valid complaints and remember the role they play in the lives of many children. Witnessing this shift reminded me, too, of how scary it can be to see another person lose hope, particularly when it is someone in a position of power or authority.

Still, the capacity to sustain hope depends on what that word engaged. We also talked about attending to children's present tense, and not just who or how they are in the future. Some children are thinking about what the world will look like when they grow up, but some are much more interested in what is happening next to them or in front of them right now: this is no less valuable just because it is immediate.

When it was my turn to present, after a conversation about Jonathan's statements, I spoke about my long-held belief in the power of despair, of dwelling with others in negative affect.

Much of what I have written previous to this project has been about the importance of sadness, anger, and even turning away from hope in some educational contexts. In my teaching and scholarship, I have struggled against mandates for always being positive, maintaining a growth mindset, believing in this cheerful, utopian future for all of us if only we try hard enough. Along with many queer theorists and some in childhood studies, I have argued for the philosophical value of letting sadness and other negative emotions fester, because they can sometimes be politically and personally true, and because the human condition is not a particularly cheerful one.

In that conversation, I was a bit of a killjoy. This is a position I do not necessarily mind. One of my academic role models, Sara Ahmed (2023), describes the figure of the killjoy as a feminist, critically minded thinker who helps orient discussions in more honest, aware directions. It is something I do naturally, and my academic training has furthered the tendency. Why be happy, the killjoy asks, when the world is so sad? I still maintain that it is important for teachers – for all of us – to remember that some of the bulletin board positivity and mandated mindfulness that goes on in schools is a veneer that ignores the daily experiences of many children, teachers, and families. Having a consistent critical mindset can help a teacher excel.

But on that day, after I left the Zoom and walked into my kitchen to boil pasta for my family, my children having spent much of the day on their own Google meets, the floors covered with grime, KN95 masks strewn on the counter, and my wife just home from a long day at her clinic, I thought, "Do I really mean what I said? Do I really mean that I want to find ways to live without hope, or am I just scared of running out of reasons to have it?"

The more I thought about it, the more I agreed with Jonathan. To face a child without hope isn't so much wrong as it is impossible. Children are not "the future," they are the right now just as much as any of us. But, there is just enough truth in the romantic vision of children as the future, that when we turn toward them, which is something I love and want to keep doing, we have to do it with hope.

Increasingly, as much as I think it is a combination of privilege and delusion that results in the excess positivity we see in schools and classrooms, I also find overwhelming negativity rooted in privilege and delusion. It ignores the material reality of children's moment-to-moment lives: their hunger, their longing for touch, their tripping over themselves and each other, their sounding out lists of words. None of these things can happen adequately in a state of shock and despair, so those of us who face children have to do it with hope. Even when we do, though, even when we reach into whatever internal resources we have and try to find that hope, the understanding of what is happening around us – the possibilities of different kinds of bleakness, malaise, and catastrophe facing our world – these things impact the way we interact with each other, the things we want from one another. Because of this, it matters to think about what it means to be close to another person in the midst of existential despair. When the surrounding conditions are frightening, dangerous, and destructive, how can we still have relationships? How can a teacher relate to a child with integrity and still acknowledge the damage adults have wrought, are wreaking, on children's worlds? How do we face each other every day in schools and classrooms seeking out connection when we know just how hard authentic relationships are to come by in a world that can feel like it is ending?

## Masks, Smoke, and Inhalers

*It is very cold outside today as I make my way to Ainsley's classroom. When I come in, Ainsley smiles up at me. So does Teenie. "Lots of us are out sick today!" Teenie exclaims. I notice that the classroom is indeed sparsely populated, and Ainsley affirms what Teenie has said, "That's right, Teenie." Teenie looks pleased to win her teacher's* approval. "There are a lot of germs going around right now, and a lot of our friends are home sick, I think." Then she looks at me, "Let's hope we don't get it!" she laughs.

The children are ostensibly playing a phonics game, but the topic of germs spreading has provoked them. Conrad speaks up, "My mom still wears a mask to the store," he says, "from when there was COVID." I quickly calculate: Conrad was born in 2016, so for him, COVID mainly happened around ages 4–5.

"Oh yeah!" Teenie says. "My mom does that sometimes too when she goes to the store."

"I remember COVID!" Josie interjects excitedly.

"I remember that thing!" calls Zed. Soon all the children are chattering excitedly, mainly just confirming again and again that they remember what COVID is. Some are telling stories about times they were sick with it, others just remembering seeing others in their world wearing masks. "And there's hand sanitizer!" one child says; so many are chattering at once I can't even identify who.

"And there's those tests, you stick them up your nose," Josie adds, "And there's shots."

This seems a more somber thought for the room. "Shots," someone repeats. For a moment, there is quiet. Ainsley seems poised to return to the lesson she originally planned. Before she does, though, Josie speaks again, more quietly this time. "My mom got that and it was hard to breathe, not me though."

I hear several children inhale loud and deep, exercising their own ability to breathe. I become conscious of my own breathing, too. Mickey, exhaling, remarks, "The smoke from summer makes it hard to breathe too."

"You don't wear a mask for that one," says Lyuba.

Ainsley, listening closely to the children, clarifies. "Are you talking about last summer? I remember that too." She looks at me as though for confirmation. "Were you around?" Ainsley speaks to me directly, something she almost never does when I am observing. "There was the wildfire smoke." I nod, remembering those days clearly: several hot weeks in early summer when asthmatics like me, and, apparently,

Mickey, couldn't safely go outside. "That was very hard," Ainsley says, nodding toward Mickey.

"I did too wear a mask," Mickey says, addressing Lyuba, "I did!"

"Oh," Lyuba says, a bit chastened, "I didn't, Mickey, I just… I didn't wear the mask for that but I wore it for the COVID."

The emotional tone in the room feels really low. Several kids are still breathing loudly in and out, as though thinking through the various possible obstacles between them and their air. Ainsley opens her mouth again as though to say something, then seems to change her mind. "All right," she says, and clears her throat, "Let's go back to our rhyming."

This episode felt so painful and real to me. Of course, Ainsley and I have lived through the same recent chapters that all the children have, and we have had to adjust our worldviews accordingly. Sometimes it feels a lot like being a child, making those adjustments. Okay, we learn, there can be a global pandemic that totally upends life as we know it. Before 2020, I honestly had no idea that could happen! This must feel so much like learning that the scrawls of lines and loops on a page can actually mean you're supposed to make a sound, or like learning that a teacher can call your mom and totally change how your afternoon goes. Okay, the fires in Canada can get so bad that an amateur gardener in Massachusetts has to take steroids just to go outside and water her plants. This was news to me, too!

At first blush, the children in Ainsley's class may appear to be confused about these different episodes of world events encroaching on their own and their families' lives, conflating them in a way that isn't entirely accurate, just because of the organ systems they touch. But when I thought about it, I realized they were ultimately no more confused about the whole thing than I was. It is painful, and it is also just the reality they are assimilating to, not knowing first-hand any other. Sometimes, when I am having trouble breathing, I'm also not totally sure why. It's hard to be a person!

How is Ainsley meant to react to this kind of confusion, suffering, and grief? What does it do to her ability to relate to these children, that the world she is offering them is one where they sometimes can't breathe? Ainsley didn't construct this world, but she has been in it longer, and sometimes she feels a lot of responsibility for it. I feel this too, facing those younger than I am. I imagine many adults do, though plenty respond only by growing increasingly defensive.

The moments the children share with each other here: Zed, Lyuba, Mickey, all the little breathing bodies – they are raw, authentic, poignant, maybe helpful. There is something shared among them. In this sense, the very pain and chaos of their world breeds closeness. There is hope in that – that in the midst of sorrow and confusion, there can be opportunities for richer human connection. Ainsley stands a bit outside of that solidarity, tasked with the difficulty not only of keeping the curriculum flowing, but, more pressingly, of justifying what can feel like an unjustifiable reality. That job feels untenable to her, it seems, and so she makes the understandable move of changing the subject. Let's get back to work. What else is a teacher supposed to do?

## All That Tech

A lot of adults who don't spend significant amounts of time in contemporary elementary schools are surprised by how much time children in most public schools spend using technology. This is something that was gradually shifting for a long time before the pandemic. Newly available technologies, mandates that children become more adept in STEM fields from an early age, teacher shortages, grants and political pressure to orient children increasingly toward computer mediated learning, and the sheer addictive power of the screen: all of these things have played their roles. Then, of course, children across the United States were learning from home for months on end, and technology was a savior. It enabled some aspects of curriculum and even interpersonal connection to keep going. Teachers had to lean heavily on educational technology to do their jobs at all.

I am not sure why so much of it stuck once children returned to school buildings. Partly, perhaps, because we had already been moving in that direction, and partly because such a sudden, seismic change in education is unusual enough that when it happens, it is hard to change back. Also, many teachers saw specific advantages to educational technologies. The one I see enacted most often is that putting three-quarters of a class of children on a computer screen enables the teacher to work directly and effectively with the other quarter of the class. Of course, many teachers have long arranged their classrooms this way, but it does seem like few activities are as effective at keeping children occupied without disruption as those mediated by a screen.

I am old fashioned, I know, in thinking that the disruptions that happen when, say, a teacher asks most of the class to play analog math games or write in journals together while she works with a small group of their peers, are preferable to the endless rounds of Lexia, ST Math, i-Ready, and innumerable other programs children are constantly plugged into. Most of the teachers I talk to estimate that children in their classes spend about two thirds of most school days using tech, which, conservatively, comes to three or four hours a day. That is a lot, and few families are alert to that amount; it's a change that happened without a whole lot of public input. It would be bizarre if that level of engagement with technology *didn't* have an impact on human relationships, including between students and teachers. This observation from Benjamin and Laila's classroom offers one glimpse into what I think can be the technological dystopia of many elementary schools today.

*Benjamin was out all of last week recovering from a minor surgery. He came back Monday even though Laila told him it was fine to take more time, and then he promptly got sick with COVID and had to stay home for longer. Laila misses him, and she knows the children do too. It's always hard to teach alone, she tells me, remembering other experiences she's had, but there's something even harder about it when you're used to working with a partner. She stopped by Benjamin's house to leave a basket of cookies outside, and she has been, at his request, sending him photos and updates on what is happening in their class.*

*When I get to the classroom, my first impression is that things are running quite smoothly, especially considering that one of the teachers is absent. Laila is sitting at her usual horseshoe table in the corner, working with a small group of children. Other than her gentle voice and the occasional utterances of the children in her group, the room is entirely silent. It looks very orderly: nothing on the floor, nothing out of place, children in their seats.*

*Looking a little more closely helps me understand what is enabling this order. About six kids are sitting at their desks, headphones on, playing Lexia, a phonics program with several game-like features. Another two are leaning against the walls at the back of the room, also wearing headphones, these plugged into iPads offering instructional videos about finding the main idea in a passage. The rest of the students are sitting around the table where Benjamin usually teaches his small groups. Each of them is also wearing headphones, some with Chromebooks, others with iPads, each doing some kind of literacy game or exercise, no two looking at the same thing.*

*Another teacher pops her head in to check on how things are going, understanding that Laila is in a different situation from usual with Benjamin out. She sees the order in the room, smiles, and glances at me. "Thank goodness for all that tech!" she says and makes her way along down the hall.*

Laila's students were on technology slightly more than usual because of Benjamin's absence, but actually, the students in co-taught classrooms tend to use tech less than others overall for the same reason. Once we know technology is there, it is so easy to use it as a babysitter. Certainly I have struggled with this in my parenting life as well. Nothing quite keeps a child still and quiet like plugging them into a gamified screen and putting earphones on their head.

I do not mean to sound like a terrible bore, moaning about the evils of technology. I understand the opportunities it affords for children to learn at their own pace and, sometimes, really have fun while drilling down on an otherwise dull set of skills. I certainly understand the temptation of using tech to quiet the room and enable the deep teaching that can happen during uninterrupted small-group instruction.

Yet there is something dystopic to me about the scene I saw in Laila's classroom that day, the scenes I am growing so familiar with in classrooms I visit regularly. It is alienating to have things run so smoothly specifically because no two people are doing the messy work of engaging directly with one another. How can children and teachers have relationships when this is the nature of their world? When does technology become a problematic third object mediating these connections, and is there any hope for doing anything about it?

If there is someone to "blame" in the exceptional amount of technology being used in elementary and early childhood classrooms, though, it certainly is not the individual teacher. Later, when I spoke to Laila about my observation, she felt chagrined and sad. "I know," she says,

> I lean on it more than usual when Benjamin is out, but the sad part is, that's actually how much the district *wants* us to be using it. So actually, my kids are getting caught up when that happens... like, they're finishing all these assessments and levels and what have you, that they were expected to be done with back in October.

Ainsley had a similar perspective on technology. "I don't know," she said,

> if it's really worth the trade offs, because it definitely gets in the way. Some of the times that they are on Chromebooks and all of those things, they are definitely learning, but a lot of times I think we would be better off just playing with each other or joking around or something. That's what a lot of them crave, sometimes they don't even know how much they crave it. But the truth is,

we don't have a choice. We have to put this stuff in front of them, we have to get them to a certain level, or else we get called out for it.

One complexity about using technology this way is, of course, that it enables significantly greater surveillance over what teachers are doing with their students. Because of the way a lot of online instructional programs work, a district official can easily find out which teacher has had which student on which program for what amount of time per week. Without any skepticism from most school leaders about the utility and benefits of tech for young children, it just becomes another "gotcha" for teachers. It is part of the educational world they are participating in without much will, and then the children in their classes also become participants with no choice at all.

By making this happen, not only are we enforcing this somewhat eerie vision: a room filled with children, each plugged into their own device – we are also showing children that a computer can just as easily do the trick, and the teacher, in fact, is sometimes little more than servant to the master that is tech. It is silly to think that this, along with all of the other details of the world where they are living, would not impact children's visions of relationships with their teachers.

I found myself heartened that in my individual conversations with children about closeness and relationships, no one brought up technology. Two children mentioned the cuddly, close feeling of watching television with a sibling or caregiver, but no one specifically named technology as something to have a relationship with. No one drew a computer, robot, or iPhone in any of their illustrations. I think this is important to remember: that as much as children can seem to be part of the addiction most of us struggle with on some level, they don't see it as taking the place of human connection, at least not yet. It will be interesting, as AI continues to evolve and more children have opportunities to interact with it in different forms, to see how this aspect of relationships changes.

## Anxiety and Closeness

Though no child drew or discussed technology during our interviews, several children did bring up anxiety in direct relation to conditions in the world around them. Ainsley's student Owen described liking his time in school "because there isn't stuff to worry about here."

I asked Owen what kinds of things he worries about outside of school. He told me, "oh, just this and that, the things that are happening, the things the grownups are worrying."

He was nonspecific, so I pushed a little more, "Are the grownups in your house worried a lot of the time?" "Oh yeah," said Owen, his tone quite casual, "They're worried on the news, they're worried on dinner, they're worried." He paused. "They're worried the money, they're worried the things at work, it's like they just worry and worry and worry worry worry." Owen started biting his nails as he described the stress around him. I said that it sounded like he really pays attention to how the adults around him are feeling. Then I asked Owen who he feels close to, and he mentioned his foster parents and his sister. "I like cuddling with her in the morning, she's very tiny." At school, though, he likes "Ms. Robyns because like I was saying, she stays happy, she loves us."

It was interesting to think about Ainsley as someone Owen could feel close to because she represents an unworried adult. Ainsley thinks of herself as someone who worries a lot, not least about the students she cares for so much. She knows the conditions in their worlds can be extremely difficult, and she approaches that knowledge with generosity.

Among other things, Ainsley tries to use the small periods of unstructured play she is able to grant children to understand more about their lives. "Students will reveal things about themselves and their lives in the roles they have when they play," she told me. Describing Owen particularly, she said,

> I witnessed him playing the role of a parent throwing a baby doll across the room and telling the baby, "you are bad." Then he ran after the baby in a new role as a brother, saying "I will help you baby, I love you." It taught me so much about Owen, I wish we had more time like that. We witness and learn so much about students in those kinds of unstructured play settings.

Ainsley knows how much stress Owen is coping with in his family and in relation to the various issues facing him as a person in the world. She also knows very well that Owen is not the only child in her class dealing with life's difficulties and specifically the challenges associated with being a child who lives in poverty in 2020s America. Much of what Owen has had to take on is specific to being a child living in poverty, in a town surrounded by other children living in poverty and many adults who are dealing with food insecurity, housing insecurity, and drug addiction. And some of what he has had to take on is just about being a child and dealing with development.

Ainsley wishes she had more time to know these specifics about her students and support them in working through them. She also knows that what she gets or interprets in school is only ever going to be one version of a child's complicated story, mediated through her own lens and assumptions. She told me on a separate occasion,

> I can assume a child has a tougher life when they come in with the same outfit every day, or I can assume that a child's parents are neglectful when they never have a snack, or they send the child to school without the proper snow gear… and sometimes I'm sure the assumptions are not too far from the truth… but it's all so hard to know. A child may come into school with the same outfit because a parent is having a hard time paying for new clothes,

but that outfit may be washed every night. A child may not come into school with a snack because they are eating it on the bus on the way to school…

I asked Ainsley how often children tell her specific things about their lives outside of school, like Owen's description of all the worry that surrounds him. Ainsley answered,

Many of my students do reveal things about their lives, but it is also hard to decipher their stories at this age. Unless they are explicitly saying 'my adult hits me' or 'my adult doesn't bring me to school because they sleep in,' I try my best to just really pay attention to what they tell me, to keep track of patterns. I can know everything about their lives but also know nothing at all.

Somewhere in the midst of saying this, Ainsley started to doubt herself.

I hope that makes sense… I also try my best to be sensitive to what a child tells me whether it is the truth or distorted. Even if their truth is distorted it is still their truth. It is still how they are feeling in that moment.

Ainsley's explanation did make sense to me, partly because of its built-in contradictions. I took it as an example of how sometimes the challenges of the world, the feeling that there are so many problems that we are all encountering all the time, can actually bring children and teachers closer together. There is tremendous compassion in Ainsley's statement. Even though the requirements of her job might sometimes pull her away from her best judgment in terms of giving children the time and space they need to work through their struggles, her compassion helps her present that unworried, stable, and happy figure Owen needs and describes. Sharing in the pain around them brings them closer. Is it possible for that to always be the way? Would that be desirable? Honestly, I am not sure.

## The Thing About Uncertainty

The thing about uncertainty is that it offers little satisfaction. So many of the teachers I work with want to know not, "what is the nature of relationships that unfold in the classroom?" but "how can I form better relationships?" Often that question translates into, "how can I form relationships that will make my teaching life easier, make life in school and maybe even outside of school a bit easier for my students, lead to more compliance, and help children learn more, faster?"

Mainly, we all know that if an easy answer existed to that question, we would have it by now. But we keep searching for it, and it is sometimes in that search that rich, funny, poignant, and meaningful moments between one person and another or among a group of students emerge. Of course, it is also sometimes in that search that frustration and burnout occur, or relationships sour.

The thing about uncertainty, too, is that whether we like it or not, and crucially, whether we admit it or not, it is a state all of us exist in most of the time. When it comes to understanding what the future holds for each of us, our families, the children we teach and the other people we feel close to, much less the planet we inhabit, uncertainty has come to occupy a substantial part of many people's consciousness. In the US, there is renewed uncertainty about the nature of our government, something many of us grew up at least partly taking for granted. Goodness knows the pandemic brought both medical and economic uncertainty for many of us. The uncertainty of our shared climate looms ever-present, affecting all of us differently but not really leaving anyone untouched. Many of us have had to adjust to being less sure than we might have thought we were entitled to be. It is not an easy thing.

The thing about uncertainty is, though, that even at its worst, its most anxious, it does allow for beauty and connection. There is great power in admitting to a child that not only do we not know everything, we actually don't know much at all. It is not a power that automatically cements a relationship, but it is a power that allows for more curiosity. It also allows children to figure out the level of connection, and the language about connection, that will work for them. No one benefits from the adult pretense that we know everything is okay in the world or in every child's life. Similarly, no one benefits from a mirage that adults understand everything about how closeness works.

So often, Ainsley, Benjamin, and Laila struggle to make things work a particular way in their classroom, and their students struggle right there beside them. Both classrooms are places of joy, confusion, chaos, learning, anger, exhaustion, relationship, and alienation. Most classrooms are like that much of the time: all the things at once, not sure what they are. Children, teachers, everyone is trying, but no one really knows what to do. Isn't that just a microcosm of the rest of our lives together? Might we all feel a little steadier if we let it, let each other, be, instead of trying to figure it all out?

## Closing with Questions

As you finish this chapter and this book, use these questions to help you make connections to your own practice.

- ♦ How do you think your feelings about the country and the world impact your relationships with students?

    *Sometimes, all teachers come into contact with national or global issues that have really strong emotional impacts on us: climate crises like hurricanes and wildfires, school shootings, public health emergencies that close or change the nature of school or necessitate genuinely difficult interactions. When this happens to you, or when big, complicated issues come up in curriculum or class discussion, how do you see it impacting your relationships with your students? What are some times that you can remember working to put your feelings about big issues aside, and how did that pan out for you? How do other teachers you know handle this complexity of the job?*

♦ What do you do when what the school or district asks of you is different from your own beliefs about what constitutes good practice? What do you think teachers *should* do about this?

*Ainsley, Benjamin, and Laila struggle with how the mandates they face from their districts around curriculum, timing, and technology go against what they wish they could do with their students, or what they think would be best. What are some times that you have found yourself in similar positions, and how do you handle it? Should teachers push back against these kinds of mandates? How do you see that kind of resistance panning out?*

♦ What are some of the ways you have seen children express uncertainty about the society they are in, or the issues facing the world, through their behavior in the classroom?

*Sometimes, children are so aware of what is happening in the world around them, and inevitably it impacts their emotions and behavior. We see this in the poignant conversation Ainsley has with her students about COVID, which then turns to issues around how climate impacts their health. What are some times that you have heard children talk about world or national issues? How do you think your students' awareness of the world impacts their feelings and behavior in school? How does it impact their ways of relating to you as an adult?*

♦ What does it mean to you to have hope as a teacher, and how can you help yourself sustain that hope amidst largescale uncertainty?

*As you wrap up this book, reflect on the things you are uncertain about: in your life, in your teaching, in the country and in the world. See what it feels like to allow yourself to stay with that uncertainty. What does "hope" mean to you specifically in relation to that uncertainty? How can you bring that hope into your teaching, and how can you help children, as well as other teachers, find ways to do that for themselves as well?*

# Reference

Ahmed, Sara. *The Feminist Killjoy Handbook: The Radical Potential of Getting in the Way*. Seal Press, 2023.

For Product Safety Concerns and Information please contact our EU representative GPSR@taylorandfrancis.com
Taylor & Francis Verlag GmbH, Kaufingerstraße 24, 80331 München, Germany

www.ingramcontent.com/pod-product-compliance
Lightning Source LLC
Chambersburg PA
CBHW070402240426
43661CB00056B/2509